MW01269093

# TAKE BACK YOUR DREAMS

PRIORITIZE YOUR PURPOSE, REGAIN CONTROL OF
YOUR TIME, AND CREATE THE LIFE YOU WANT
BEFORE IT'S TOO LATE

SANDY DEMPSEY

# ADVANCE PRAISE

"You don't have to be the victim of your world. You can be the architect of your life. Sandy shows you how to build the life of your dreams, step by step, in her new book."

"Sandy masterfully weaves together her expertise as an executive, life coach, and healer to create a practical step-by-step guide to living your dream life! Not only does Sandy empower us with her shed of tools, but she offers us healing through the energetic blueprint of her words. After each reading, I felt nourished and inspired like I had spent an afternoon with a good friend and a cup of tea. I can't wait to start implementing Sandy's guidance and watch my life change!

"Sandy Dempsey's book Take Back Your Dreams takes us through a step-by-step process of self-love, self-honor and self-respect so we can create the lives of our secret longings."

"Sandy is an inspirational guide on the journey of life and living your dreams. She models for her clients the tools and techniques she shares in her book, Take Back Your Dreams. In other words, Sandy walks her talk."

"Take Back Your Dreams is both inspirational and empowering. Sandy not only shares a roadmap to help you create the life you most want, but she also provides tools and techniques to take care of your Self along the way."

"The title says it all and delivers every word of it – clearly and easily. Sandy exemplifies her own advice by breaking goals and targets down into manageable baby steps. Each chapter is a wealth of information delivered in bite size chunks in a specific and organized order as a guide to get exactly what you want out of your life. An easy read in one sitting – but to get all that is delivered you will have to take action and will want to revisit certain chapters over and over as you steadily grow into the life you want to create."

"In Take Back Your Dreams, Sandy draws upon her vast breadth of knowledge and personal life experiences to provide valuable life-transforming tools for anyone who is ready to take the leap into the life of their dreams."

— THE REV. JENNIFER C. NELSON,
ENVIRONMENTAL SCIENTIST AND
DEACON, CALIFORNIA, USA

"Identifying our innermost dreams can be the hard part, knowing what we truly want out of life. But once you have identified that dream, Sandy Dempsey's action plan will be instrumental in helping you to realize that dream."

— C. MCNABB, RETIREE, WASHINGTON
STATE, USA

"Are you looking to make a big career change – or life change? Sandy's new book is a guide for busy women who want to pursue their dreams and make them reality with very easy step-by-step tools that help you take control of your life & time.  She leads by example and shares the tools and techniques she uses to inspire and empower her clients. As someone who changed their career path mid-life - this book has a lot of tools and resources to help you on your journey and keep you focused on the end goal. Her book was such a great read and so relatable. There were so many moments throughout her book I kept thinking, 'Yes, I so agree with that'! Take Back Your Dreams is inspirational and worth the read.  If your dream doesn't scare you – it's not big enough! Sandy will help you not only envision your dream but help you on your path."

— LYNETTE SMITH, CERTIFIED
PROFESSIONAL PORTRAIT
PHOTOGRAPHER, WASHINGTON
STATE, USA

"Take Back Your Dreams is thought-provoking, insightful, motivating, and inspiring. I believe it will help anyone who is ready to live a meaningful and joyful life."

"After reading Sandy's new book I feel empowered and ready to start achieving my life's purpose and dreams! The concepts and strategies laid out in each chapter made me realize that my lifelong goals are actually achievable. I am excited to take the leap and go after my true calling in life!"

"Sandy is a master storyteller. As 'weird' as it may sound, the stories actually help you understand the framework she teaches."

"Take Back Your Dreams spoke to me on so many levels. I am finally able to put my targets and dreams as a priority. It's ok to say no and embrace the self-care that I have been neglecting. Allowing myself to come first will help me reach the life I always envisioned. The amount of insight I gained from this book is immeasurable."

"It's common to hear people who intend to create change in their lives – physically, mentally, and emotionally – refer to their efforts as 'doing the work.' However, doing the work is rarely easy. It requires strong commitment, focused intent, and meticulous introspection. As the reader, we want you to know that we fully support Sandy's ability to help you on your journey. The tools Sandy offers in this book are invaluable for unlocking your creative potential and your soul's calling. They provide just a taste of what she has to offer, and if you are blessed to go deeper with her, the rewards can be immeasurable."

"Take Back Your Dreams by Sandy Dempsey is your roadmap to reinvention. There was nothing like a worldwide pandemic to make people sit alone and think about those unfulfilled dreams. Even afterward, you may ask how to get from the dream stage to the living your dream stage. Take Back Your Dreams by Sandy Dempsy is a book for anyone who is reinventing their life or for those who just need a pivot. She uses real-life clients and relatable personal stories. Moreover, she understands that people have secret lifelong dreams, but the imagined obstacles hold them back from even trying to go after what they want. A long-time life coach, Sandy Dempsy provides some tips on how to prioritize your values, while still going after your dreams. In addition, she shares how to use visualization, goals and targets, and small steps to achieve those life-long dreams. Sandy includes journal questions to help you along the way, as well as tips and suggestions to help make those important changes that will empower you to overcome obstacles, and not let them keep you from your dreams."

— GEORGIA MAKITALO, WRITER AND HOST
OF THE PRE-RAPHAELITE MUSE PODCAST,
MINNESOTA, USA

# CONTENTS

*For my loving husband Bob.*
*You were my lifelong companion and my biggest supporter.*
*Your love, support and encouragement always gave me space*
*to fly.*
*You gave me the courage to live my dreams.*
*I am holding you in my heart until our souls meet again.*

# THE OVERWHELM IS PALPABLE

R ita came to me by referral. When she first sat in the chair across from me, she could not speak. She was trying hard to contain the myriad emotions bubbling inside of her, but a few tears managed to escape, and she reached for a tissue from the box I always had readily available.

"So, what's going on here?" I asked in a gentle voice. I sincerely wanted to know.

She took a deep breath. "Nothing's going right. I feel so overwhelmed."

I waited, but she didn't say anything more. She was looking down at the tissues she held in her hands.

"Tell me more."

She sat for a long time. I patiently waited and gave her space to gather herself.

Coaching is not therapy, but before we can work together, a client needs to feel safe and she needs to be able to share what is happening, and this often involves strong emotions that had been buried for a long time. My job isn't to fix this. There is nothing wrong. Tears and strong emotions are signs of something sitting just beneath the surface ready to come out. When the tears come, I know we are close to a breakthrough.

With Rita it was no different. Her therapist had referred her to me because she knew that Rita needed support to take action toward her dreams. She kept tripping over all the things going on in her life and felt like she had no control of her time or energy.

Rita looked up at me, fiercely, and leaned forward as she shared, "I'm tired of helping everyone else meet their goals and bring their dreams to life. I have my own goals, my own dreams! I know what I want!" Her voice was strong.

Then her shoulders collapsed, and she sat back, looking down at the tissues crumpled up in her hands. "But, I feel so overwhelmed. There don't seem to be enough hours in the day or days in the week to do everything I need to, let alone the things that I want to do. I'm so tired most of the time that I just don't have the energy to work on any of my own projects, let alone create the life of my dreams."

Rita's words were laden with both unwavering determination and frustration.

Rita was about to turn fifty in a few months. She was beginning to feel like time was running out for her. She managed a local B&B after years of working the front desk at a local hotel and raising two kids. She was brilliant at her job. The guests adored her. Vendors and staff looked up to her as a force of nature. But this job wasn't Rita's dream.

She'd always dreamed of having an event planning business. She loved organizing parties, bringing people together and helping people create memorable celebrations. She did this for friends and family but had never gotten paid for it.

In the beginning, she just did it because she loved to. But the more and more events she organized, the more and more people started asking for her help. Although she hadn't admitted it to very many people, creating events lit her up. It filled her with a sense of satisfaction, purpose, and joy when she stood back as a party was winding down, watching family and friends cry, hug, and laugh as they said goodbye. If there were tears and laughter, she knew she'd done a good job.

Rita loved people and loved communities. She was a connector. If anyone needed a photographer, caterer, or someone to rent a tent, she had it covered. She always knew someone or knew someone who knew someone. It came natural to her. It did not feel like work.

Pre-pandemic, Rita and her husband, Ron, were coasting and going through the motions. During the lockdown, though, there were a lot of conversations, disagreements, tears, and eventually laughter. She felt like they were really seeing and hearing one another and building a future together.

She wanted to create something. She wanted to spend the next ten or more years doing what she loved and felt called to do. She only had so many more years left, and she wanted to make them count. Rita was done going through the motions. She wanted to wake up every day excited to face the day ahead. She wanted to live her life with purpose, and that meant starting her own event planning company.

But when things started to return to normal and Ron went back to work, he seemed to slip back into his old patterns. He wanted her to go back to work, too, maximize her 401k, and prepare to retire early so they could travel the country in their RV. She loved the idea of traveling, but not the idea of going back to the old normal.

Ron wanted life to go back to normal, which meant going out to dinner several times a week with friends and coworkers, playing pickle ball and golf together, and planning weekend travel trips in the RV.

Her kids, although grown, called almost every day to tell her all their problems or ask for advice. Her daughter was expecting her first baby, and her son was on a constant roller coaster of finding "the one" and then going through a heart-wrenching break-up. She wanted to be there for her children, but she felt over-whelmed sometimes by their neediness.

The local women's group she belonged to was plan-ning a big post-pandemic fundraising gala and just assumed she'd plan and organize the whole thing. She loved the women in her group. Normally, she would have loved to tackle such a project, but in that moment, it felt like a burden, one more thing on her plate. And if she was honest, she felt resentful that everyone had just assumed she would do it and do it for free. Plus, no one had even asked her.

With so many asks coming her way on a daily basis, Rita was frustrated and exhausted. She felt like she had no control over her time or her life. How was she going to add launching her own event planning business on top of everything else? She felt her voice drown in a sea of requests from others.

Rita's overwhelm was palpable. I could hear the hope and excitement in her voice when she told me about her goals and dreams. And I could hear all her energy wane as she recounted all the things she "must" and "ought to" do because "others were counting on her to."

I knew Rita was committed. She knew what she wanted. She was ready to reclaim her dreams, take back control of her time, and begin creating the life she wanted before it was too late.

And that is exactly what she did! Using the tools, techniques, and exercises I share in this book, Rita regained control of her life. She had the time and the energy to take action and she turned her dream of creating memorable celebrations for people into a successful event planning business. Rita started living the life she'd dreamed of for years!

# 2

# THE MEANDERING ROAD TO A LIFE OF FULFILLMENT

The rain pounded on the roof and ran down the windshield in waves as I sat in the front seat hunched over the steering wheel crying just as hard as the rain was coming down outside. I was sitting in the parking lot gearing up the courage to go inside and meet with my therapist for the first time. Wave after wave of emotions I couldn't identify washed over me. I opened the car door, threw up, grabbed a wad of tissues, and ran across the parking lot, getting drenched along the way.

I stood in the foyer breathing deep, trying to calm myself while trying to dry my face before stepping into the elevator to ride to the third floor and meet change head on.

I knew my life had to change. Nothing was working. My job, my marriage, life in general. I was overwhelmed, stressed out, and honestly, I felt like I was going crazy. Eighty-plus-hour weeks were the norm.

Being overcome by emotions I didn't understand at the most inopportune times was becoming a daily occurrence.

I couldn't continue to live my life as I had for the past thirty-plus years. All of my time and energy was devoted to my job and my family. There was never any room for me.

I had a great salary, lots of perks, and invitations to speak at national trade shows, but it all seemed dull, colorless, and soulless.

All my dreams of being a writer, working for myself, finishing my degree, going to graduate school, and making a difference in the world came back like an avalanche. I was being buried alive under long-suppressed emotions and dreams of an unlived life. I couldn't breathe. I was suffocating. I was losing my mind.

Then a surprising thing happened. I heard a voice. A wobbly, fierce, five-year-old's voice whispering to me from the darkness, *"It's not too late. You're okay. You can have a different life. You can follow your dreams. Ask for help."*

That turning point led me to my first therapist.

I knew what I wanted, what my dreams were. I wanted to write, teach, and work for myself. I wanted to express my creativity through my work. And I wanted to help others, to make a difference in the world.

But how was I supposed to go after my dreams when I had no time?

Asking for help wasn't easy. It was the antithesis of

the way I'd lived my life up until that moment. But was I really living? That first step was the hardest. As I mentioned already, I cried all the way to my first appointment, and it wasn't the last time. I had to continually find the courage to step outside of the familiar, discover who I was, separate my needs from others, identify what was important to me, name what I wanted, and take the steps to create it.

It was slow and steady progress with lots of ups, downs, and even back.

I continued working my job but was able to create boundaries that gave me more time to myself. I began to write and teach and started several side businesses that allowed me to explore ideas I'd always wanted to pursue. I dabbled, played, and began to rediscover the parts of myself that had been lost for decades.

Then I hit a new wall. Change is dynamic and doesn't stop. After walking my mom through her final transition after years of battling metastatic breast cancer, I became ill. My job had once again become more than a little stressful as a merger became a takeover and almost everyone I'd worked with for years was fired. I was one of only a handful of former employees remaining and I was being asked to work more hours and take on more responsibility for less money.

The stress of taking care of my mom for so long, even though it was something I wanted to do and was honored to do, took its toll on me physically. My job was beginning to become all-consuming again. I'd drained my savings taking care of my mom and her estate was in debt. I was scared to quit my job and not have any income. I was once again adrift, having lost sight of my dreams, my purpose, and what was important to me.

Less than a year later, I found myself having an emergency procedure and two blood transfusions to save my life. Things had to change. I needed to regain control of my time and my life once more and begin creating the life I wanted to live.

It's funny how once you make a choice and begin moving in the direction you want to go, the Universe begins to align with you.

A few weeks later, I quit my job and was on a plane flying three thousand miles across the country to see about a potential consulting job that would allow me to combine all my previous work experience with my desire to help a small company grow and expand. I had no guarantees and no promises, but I was ready for a change and committed to creating something new.

This single step resulted in buying a new home and moving to the Pacific Northwest—a lifelong dream I'd never believed was possible.

Taking on this new role was, at the time, what I thought was a dream come true, and in many ways, it was. But it was also the most challenging time period of my life and one that gave me more opportunities for personal growth than I'd expected in a single lifetime. There were many times I wanted to throw in the towel and just quit. It was harder than I ever imagined. But at the same time, a part of me understood that everything I was going through and being challenged by was what I needed. I'd asked for change and the Universe delivered.

As stressful and as time-consuming as my job was, I continued to invest in myself, and took time for self-care and introspection. My husband and I traveled frequently, taking road trips and seeing most of the western and central states. I attended workshops and retreats. I went back to school and found a new coach and healer to support me.

Then, once again, I hit a wall and faced a new health challenge. I knew that it was time to pivot once again and expand on my original dreams.

By now I knew that dreams weren't static and unmoving. To create a life worth living means continually learning, growing, and expanding, and I was ready once again to reach for more. And best of all, I was prepared and knew what I needed to do.

Change and transition are not easy. Living an unconventional life is not easy. Taking one step at a time toward a life bigger than you can even imagine in the present moment is not easy. The unknown can be scary. But I've discovered it's all worth it. It's allowed me to learn to live in and really experience the present moment and have hope for the future at the same time.

Today, I'm living a life I've always dreamed of and I'm the person I always dreamed I could be. Life can still be a challenge, but I love my life and I'm grateful that I can live my life purpose while supporting others to do the same.

# 3

# THE ROADMAP TO LIVING THE
# LIFE OF YOUR DREAMS

*"If your purpose is only about you, it has no branches. If it is only about the rest of the world, it has no roots."*

— DAWNA MARKOVA

How does this all work? What are you going to learn in this book? Why should you invest your time to read it?

Some of the things we are going to talk about you have probably heard before. You may have even used some of the tools I'm going to share. But we are going to revisit them, look at them in a new way, and help you put them into practice in a very precise sequence so that you can take back your dreams, prioritize what's important to you, regain control of your time, and create the life you want – before it's too late.

If you are like me, there are times in your life when you feel overwhelmed and when everything feels like it is out of control. This can happen the clearer and closer you get to what you want to do. It just seems like life throws every obstacle it can into your path. It's happened to me time and time again.

Feeling overwhelmed and out of control used to knock me down for months. There were times when I'd make really bad decisions when I felt like this. I was anxious and filled with fear and would do anything to feel safe again. I had no tolerance for the discomfort of feeling like all of my time was being used to support other people's agendas. I had no tools to cope with feeling out of control.

As I learned tools and techniques to help me deal with feeling overwhelmed, I began to feel in control again. It wasn't that I could control the outcome, the situation, or any of the people involved, but I learned I could control my reactions and certain aspects of the overwhelming emotions. Knowing the difference, of course, is a key, just as the Serenity Prayer teaches us.

God, grant me the serenity to accept the things I cannot change, courage to change the things I can, and wisdom to know the difference.

Using the tools and techniques I'll share with you in this book, and referencing them as needed, can shorten the amount of time you spend in overwhelm and allow you to regain control of your time. This will, in turn, allow you to create a plan to live the life of your dreams. How do I know this? Because it's worked for me and for my clients again and again.

Knowing what I want and having a plan doesn't

mean that the sailing will be smooth and easy. I can still feel overwhelmed, scared, and anxious. What I've learned is to ride the wave, sit with the feelings, not make any decisions during this time, and come back to the tools and techniques I'll share with you that help me feel in control again. I can then start making plans and taking action. The fears and anxieties may still be there, but they are more tolerable; I feel more in control and I'm confident in my decision making. This is what I want for you.

How is this book laid out?

First, I will share the four steps to regain control of your time and your life.

In Chapter 4, I'll share with you how slowing down is actually a counterintuitive way to speed things up.

In Chapter 5, we'll explore how using your values and personal life themes as a guiding light is a surprisingly easy way to make decisions and stay on track.

In Chapter 6, we will talk about delegating and sharing the load we carry, however uncomfortable it can be.

And in Chapter 7 we'll explore what support is, why you need it and how to get it.

Once you have these tools and techniques under your belt, we will be ready to move into learning the six keys to creating an effective plan of action.

In Chapter 8, we'll visualize the details of the life you want and begin fleshing out your dream.

In Chapter 9, we will take your dream and the details you envisioned from the previous chapter and see if it's the right time and the right place for you to start on them, as well as what you may need to change, let go of, or expand to do so.

In Chapter 10, we will explore the difference between goals and targets and make sure your targets are meaningful to you, measurable, achievable, and exciting.

In Chapter 11, we get down to the nitty gritty and start to create your plan of action by breaking things down into small steps. We'll explore two different techniques to do this.

In Chapter 12, we'll look at what happens when things don't go right, when we fall down, and when we take missteps.

In Chapter 13, our final step to creating an effective action, we'll explore what it's like to expand our vision even more so that our dreams keep growing and we can continue living the life we want.

Before we finish up together, in Chapter 14, we will dive into the slippery slope of going back to "normal."

At the end of each chapter, I'll provide an exercise or two, questions to explore in your journal, and a few tips and techniques to help you apply what we've covered in the chapter.

# 4

# SELF-CARE – THE COUNTERINTUITIVE FIRST STEP TO TAKE BACK CONTROL OF YOUR TIME

*"Self-care means listening to all your needs – physical, emotional, mental, and spiritual – and fulfilling those needs. It means living a balanced life in harmony with all parts of yourself. It requires that you discover the ways in which you deny and neglect yourself."*

— LUCIA CAPACCHIONE, PHD

Self-care is the very first step to taking back control of your time and your life. You are probably thinking *"And, just how am I supposed to do that? I feel out of control now and have no time for myself!"*

That's exactly what Jody said when she first came to see me. She was working sixty-plus hours a week as a marketing coordinator for a small boutique chain of natural food stores and traveling two weeks out of every month. Her time off was spent cooking, cleaning, prioritizing time with her husband and friends, and helping her daughter launch her own construction company. She felt pulled in a million different directions, helping everyone else but never having time for herself.

She was also worried about her health. She'd gained about twenty pounds in the last year. She tried to convince herself it was just the inevitable weight gain due to age and the hormonal changes associated with perimenopause, but her recent lab work and physician's warnings suggested otherwise. She needed to start taking better care of herself.

When I asked Jody what she wanted, she just shrugged her shoulders. With a little more prompting, she gave some generic answers about feeling better, losing weight, having more time, and having more fun. Then, as we continued to talk, she shared that what she really wanted was to share her knowledge about grassroots marketing with local small businesses to help her community grow. When I asked her to tell me more, her passion and enthusiasm was contagious. I was excited by the vivid picture she painted of a future where she was doing exactly what she loved in ways that were helping others. Her dream felt so real I was ready to hire her on the spot!

Jody knew what she wanted but was feeling so overwhelmed with the demands on her time she didn't know where to start or what to do.

I knew Jody could regain control of her time, and I knew she could create the life she'd described to me.

And I told her so. She wasn't convinced, especially when I told her the first thing we were going to work on together was self-care.

Self-care is the foundation for creating the life you want. It puts you at the center of your own life. Imagine tossing a pebble into a lake. What happens? From the center, ripples flow outward. You are the pebble. When you make yourself a priority and take care of yourself, your life begins to flow outward in all directions – effortlessly.

## SLOW DOWN TO SPEED UP

For me, the meaning of self-care may have changed in some of the details over the years, but the three basic features have always remained the same – time alone to read, journal, and reflect. That was until one day when I could no longer see well enough to read or write, and I had to completely redefine what self-care was.

I'd already committed to taking better care of myself and to practice self-care. The first step was to combine the support of allopathic medicine with my complementary and alternative health care practices, including diet and lifestyle, because what I was doing wasn't working. It wasn't that I didn't feel well occasionally; I didn't feel good most of the time.

After seeing a new doctor, I decided that although I'd always been against taking medication, it was the right choice to support my overall health and well-being. That's when it felt like everything fell apart.

Within twenty-four hours of beginning the new medication, I was suddenly unable to see well enough to read and write. I couldn't believe it. Here I was focused on self-care and suddenly the foundation of my self-care routine – reading and writing – was taken away from me. I felt like I was being tested, or pushed, to surrender –to what, I didn't know.

Then I was angry. Why was this happening to me? How could I make self-care a priority if I couldn't read and write?

Then I started to pray and ask for guidance, and not in an unattached way – I wanted to make a deal with the Universe. Let me read and write again, and I'll never eat another piece of chocolate.

That didn't work.

Then I was overcome with a deep sadness and felt sorry for myself. I still didn't understand why it happened.

The reason I was put on the medication resolved itself, and after three weeks, I no longer had to take the medication. Still, I feared the damage had been done, and I'd never be able to read and write with ease again.

Friends reminded me there were audiobooks and speech-to-text apps, but if you are not a reader, then you wouldn't understand. Audiobooks are great, and I listen to them in my car all the time, but it's not the same. I don't retain the information in the same way from an audiobook as I do from reading the words on the page of a book. Plus, it's a tactile thing; feeling the book in my hands, holding it, smelling it – all contributes to the relaxation of my body and my mind.

My doctor told me to wait eight to twelve weeks and then see an eye doctor for a new prescription. He promised the condition wasn't permanent, but my eyes needed time to adjust.

*Now what do I do?* I thought to myself. *I have to take care of myself physically, emotionally, intellectually, and spiritually. How do I begin? Where do I start?*

I had to accept that reading and writing weren't going to be a part of this next phase of my life and that I had to find other ways to support myself, a new self-care routine.

At first, it was super hard. I couldn't settle down. I kept trying to read and failing. It was just too hard on my eyes.

Then I started to realize that I never stop. I never just stop and *do* nothing. I always read with a purpose. Yes, it is relaxing, but I read 99 percent of the time to learn something new, to help me solve a problem, to discover a new insight, or to research something I'm curious about. I keep a list of the books I read and make summary notes about why I liked it or didn't like it, what I learned, what I'd tell other people about the book, and so on. I don't just read to read, to relax.

I had to really slow down and stop and ask myself: What do I need in this moment?

The surprising answer, although in hindsight it shouldn't have been a surprise, was *rest*. I just needed to rest. I needed to sleep, and I needed to just take some time to lie around and do nothing.

This wasn't easy. All kinds of superego thoughts rose up to punish me: "You're lazy. How do you expect to succeed if you are just lying around doing nothing? You're going to end up broke and homeless if you keep this up!" Oh my gosh, the thoughts I pummeled myself with were ruthless.

You know that superego voice? We all have it; it's the authority voice we internalized – parents, teachers, caregivers, and similar – who sits in our heads and criticizes and judges us.

I sat with the thoughts and the emotions that came with them – fear, sadness, anger. I realized that my whole life I was trying to prove to myself and everyone around me how good and valuable I was by working harder than anyone else, always contributing more than expected, always going above and beyond. A big part of my self-worth was tied to how much I did for others and now I was focused on myself.

I had to make myself a priority if I wanted to heal my body. The health challenges were real and could progress to a life-threatening situation if I didn't focus on taking care of myself.

And it wasn't just my internal thoughts beating me up. The people around me didn't understand why I was suddenly doing nothing and doing less for them. If I wasn't working, why wasn't I doing more around the house? If I wasn't working around the house, why wasn't I doing more at the office? If I had the time, why wasn't my school project complete? If I was taking all this down time, why wasn't I focused on filling my client hours?

Not only did I have to slow down, I had to take a hard look at how I actually spent my time, and I had to start saying no to other people, projects, and activities that drained my energy.

Not everyone understood, even when I explained that my health was a priority. Holding boundaries became a must.

## BOUNDARIES

Holding my boundaries was difficult at first as I always wanted to be there for everyone. However, I began to notice that after spending time with some of the people in my life, or just talking to them, I felt drained, angry, or sad afterward. I wasn't able to be myself in the relationship. The conversation was usually all about them, they dumped all their anger, frustration, and emotional upset on me, and/or they droned on and on about current events and everything terrible happening in the world.

It was hard at first, but I began to spend less and less time with these people. When they called, I didn't answer. I'd text later and just say I was too busy to talk and to message me if it was urgent. Most of the time, what they wanted to share was too much to text so they just let it go. If they wanted to get together, I said I had other plans. Over time, as it became easier to say no and hold my boundaries, I didn't make excuses and didn't feel the need to explain myself, I just said no.

I also began to look at new projects, events, and activities in a new way. I asked myself: Do I really have time for this right now? Does it light me up? If I were to take on this project, what am I willing to give up? How does this help me create the future I want for my life?

Sometimes, I'd say yes and take on something new, but after sitting with it and asking myself these questions, more often than not, I'd say no.

Holding my boundaries; saying no to the people, projects, and activities that drained my energy; and saying yes to those that inspired me and made me feel excited to get out of bed in the morning was the beginning of making myself a priority. Eventually, I had to create a new self-care routine, one focused on not just the emotional and mental aspects of my life – as I did with reading, journaling, and reflecting – but on the physical and spiritual aspects of my life.

I started going to bed earlier, and if I woke up too early, instead of getting up and starting to check emails and go through my to-do list, I gave myself permission to go back to bed. I was taking the pressure off myself to perform and giving myself the space to rest.

I watched movies and revisited some of my favorites. I have always loved movies, but in recent years, I'd just have them on in the background as I worked away on my laptop. Now I gave myself permission to just watch the movie and enjoy it. I love everything about the movies: the music selection, how the actors and actresses bring the characters to life, the storyline, the special effects, the meaning and lessons embedded in the films, the arc of the film. I laughed, cried, and just enjoyed the experience.

Other parts of my self-care routine evolved over time: a walk through the craft store without a project in mind or the need to purchase anything; Zoom calls and phone calls with friends, especially when I couldn't see to send a text message or email; guided meditations; walks around the neighborhood and in local parks.

I also started to look at new projects, not from the perspective of doing something to prove my self-worth to someone else, but based on what would really light me up and excite me for the pure joy of creating something new. For a while, all I could do was imagine the possibilities and visualize what could be; then as my eyesight began to return, I was able to start to sketch my ideas out on paper and write about them.

Self-care is an unfolding, evolving creative process.

I realized that by slowing down I was suddenly speeding up.

Projects that were once like slugging through mud were now flowing with ease.

Solutions for problems that seemed to always keep coming back were suddenly clear,

Ideas for both my job and my private practice began to arise as if out of thin air.

I was excited and enthusiastic again. I had energy. I wasn't pushing and striving.

I was slowing down yet, felt like I was more productive and efficient, like I was speeding up. It was a completely different experience and so counterintuitive that if I hadn't temporarily lost my ability to read and write, I wouldn't have discovered it. Now I share this "secret" with all my clients.

Jody, whom I mentioned at the beginning of this chapter, was very skeptical when I told her we were going to focus on self-care as her first step to regaining control of her time and life.

First, we had to look at what she really needed in this moment. Like, many of us, she needed to rest. She wasn't getting enough sleep, so this became a priority for her.

Next, we needed to define what self-care would look like for her physically, emotionally, mentally, and spiritually. She knew that one of the things she missed was her weekly yoga classes and daily walks in the park with her best friend. These things were not just physically rejuvenating but supported her emotional, mental, and spiritual well-being.

But before Jody could add these things back into her life, she needed to figure out how she was spending her time: what was draining her energy and what she needed to let go of.


## THE TIME BANK

The first thing I had Jody work on was her time bank, which is a way to record how she spent her time. I had her choose a typical day during the week – one when she was traveling and one when she was at home – and one weekend day. I explain that it was similar to tracking her spending. I wanted her to write down everything she did. She set an alarm on her phone and stopped every hour to jot down what she was doing; who she was with; where she was at; how she felt (tired, sad, angry, happy, excited, etc.); and, on a scale of one to ten, where her energy level was.

When we reviewed her time bank, it was obvious there were some people she needed to say no to. For example, when she traveled, she often went to dinner with the coworkers she was traveling with. One night was okay, but she discovered she did not want to spend every evening with them after spending all day together. She started saying no, and either got room service or takeout and spent her time resting, reading, going for a walk, or, when possible, taking a swim in the hotel pool.

After a few weeks of saying no and fortifying her new routine, she met with her team, and to her surprise, she was more energized, she made quicker and better decisions, solutions to problems were suddenly clear, new ideas were flowing, and the whole team began to have fun again. Her overnight trips dropped from six days to four days and eventually two days as her team took on more and more responsibilities.

As Jody continued to make self-care and setting boundaries a priority, she converted her full-time marketing coordinator position into a part-time consulting role. This allowed her to begin taking on local businesses as clients to teach them grassroots marketing techniques and even managing some of their programs for them. She was traveling less, sleeping more, and lost ten pounds. By slowing down, Jody's life began to speed up – in a good way. She was excited about life again and was not only creating the life she wanted; she was living it.


JOURNAL QUESTIONS AND EXERCISES

*Exercise – The Time Bank*

Choose at least one weekday and one weekend day and record how you spend your time. Set the timer on your phone to remind you to stop and record the answers to the following questions.

• What are you doing?

• Who are you with?

• Where are you?

• How do you feel? (tired, sad, angry, happy, excited, etc.)

• Rate your energy level on a scale of one to ten

Refer to your time bank journal as you explore these journaling questions:

Self-Care Journal Questions:

• What is self-care for you? Make a list of at least three things that you'd define as supportive self-care under the categories physical, emotional, mental, and spiritual.

• What does making yourself a priority mean to you?

• How do you see it changing your life?

Boundaries Journal Questions:

• Track (observe) yourself and answer the following questions related to the scenarios below: What do you say to yourself? What emotions come up? How do you feel in your body?

• What happens when you say yes to people, projects, and activities that drain your energy?

• What happens when you say no?

• What happens when you say yes to the people, projects, and activities that light you up, inspire you, and make you feel excited to get out of bed in the morning?

• What do you say to yourself? What emotions come up? How do you feel in your body?

## TIPS AND SUGGESTIONS

• Write the journal questions and exercises listed previously in your journal using your dominant hand and answer the questions by writing with your nondominant hand.

• Try one new form of movement or exercise you've never done or haven't done in a long time and see if it's a good fit with your new self-care routine.

• Experiment with expressing your emotions with your body – move, shake your fists, yell, break some old dishes, throw rocks into a puddle. Observe yourself and see if you notice any differences.

• Ask your spiritual friends for their favorite guided meditations, music, books, and similar and try them yourself.

5

# VALUES/PERSONAL LIFE THEMES – THE SURPRISINGLY EASY SECOND STEP TO TAKE BACK CONTROL OF YOUR TIME

*"Your vocation in life is where your greatest joy meets the world's greatest need."*

— FREDERICK BUECHNER

I f you were to go back and read my journals, which I have kept since I was a preteen, you would discover a constant questioning about why I'm here. What is my life purpose? You'd also read all my questions, ideas, and exploration of how to make money, how to support myself, and how I could make a difference in the world. For me, all of these things have never been separate.

In addition to journaling, I am a voracious reader, reading upward of fifty nonfiction books a year. When I have a problem or some questions, the first place I turn to is books. While I read, I also keep a journal next to me to record my insights, ideas, stories, and emotions books always spark in me. Reading is also a source of pure pleasure and relaxation for me. It is my number-one stress reliever.

In all my readings, I've repeatedly come across the idea that the sweet spot to earning a living is where your interests, gifts, and passions intersect with what the world needs. I'm sure you've read this too.

The problem I've always been challenged by is the box where my interest, gifts, and passions fall. I have so many interests. I don't want to sound like a braggart, but I have a lot of gifts and abilities. I love a lot of different things. And I can see where the world needs many of these things.

So the problem hasn't been what do I do, but how do I choose?

How do I choose just that one thing that I love doing, I'm good at and the world needs?

How do I do that and not get bored?

How do I know which one of my "things" is the best choice to live out my life purpose, make money, and make a difference in the world?

I needed to dig a little deeper. What was the common theme in the jobs I'd held, the businesses I'd started, the work I did for free, the way I spent my time?

What were my core values? What was important to me?

I knew that no matter what, I had to be always learning and growing. I also knew that I worked best in the real world, no theories or abstract ideas for me. I was all about solving problems and finding solutions for what was going on right now in the real world. Whatever I did had to incorporate these two important life themes.

Next, in terms of values, loving kindness is a core value of mine. In every interaction I have with others, I strive to always come back to loving kindness in my words and actions. For me this means sharing what I know and what I'm learning in ways that support, entertain, and empower others.

My top three values/life themes that I use to make decisions and choices (I cheated a bit, and combined a few because (1) I have trouble following rules, even my own, and (2) for me these values and life themes go hand in hand).

1. Personal growth and learning
2. Practicality combined with creativity
3. Loving kindness

In addition to knowing my core values (listed previously), I needed a word, phrase, or quote that would capture the essence of these values, what I consider the foundation of my life purpose.

This is when I came across a quote by Helen Nearing, author of the *Good Life*.

"To grow, to learn, to experience, to contribute, to share, to be intensely in the moment in which you are living, to get the most out of everything that happens to you and to realize that we are all here to contribute and to share."

This quote has guided me for decades.

It's helped remind me of my life purpose and what my guiding values were so as to make decisions aligned with them. They are kind of like the bumpers they put up when little kids bowl to keep their balls out of the gutter. I use my values, life themes and this quote as bumpers to keep me on course so that I don't ruminate over my choices and decisions.

How does knowing this help me? Let me share a story to demonstrate.

About ten years ago the company that I had worked for, for almost seventeen years was suddenly merging. It was more of a takeover than a merger, and it was ugly. Almost everyone I worked with was laid off. I was one of the few people that they wanted to keep. My workload was increasing. My pay was decreasing. And I was miserable.

An opportunity came up to do some consulting work three thousand miles away, across the country.

I was scared. What if I said yes, and it didn't work out? How could I leave a secure job with a steady paycheck for the unknown? Could I pick up and move to the West Coast? Would my husband move with me?

Was this the right decision?

I turned to my personal life themes and values. Was there an opportunity to learn? Was there an opportunity to grow? What problem would quitting and possibly moving solve? How could I use my creativity in this new situation? What was the kindest thing I could do for myself in this moment? Was there going to be an opportunity to share my experiences?

Then I knew.

Yes, this was the right decision.

Did my fear go away? No, but it did subside (a bit, not a lot).

Were there any guarantees? No, but the decision felt like the right one because it was aligned with my life themes and values.

Could I move to the West Coast? Yes.

Did I know how? No, but I could figure it out. Lots of people move all the time.

Would my husband move with me? I'd ask, but I was pretty sure. He was retired, and we'd talked for years about moving away from New Jersey.

Even though I had no idea what was going to happen next, there were lots of possibilities.

And what was most important to me, my highest values, all were telling me that yes, this was a good decision.

Within twenty-four hours, I quit my job and was on a plane heading to the West Coast.

As I shared in Chapter 2, I did land the consulting job, and I eventually moved, with my husband, to Washington State.

## KNOW YOURSELF TO KNOW THE RIGHT DECISION

When Janet and I first started working together, she'd already retired from two careers and was ready to move on to her third. She'd worked as an elementary school teacher for more than two decades before working as a corporate trainer for another twenty. Janet loved to teach, and at sixty-three years old, she wanted to teach workshops and seminars to help women transition into new careers and to empower them to take control of their future.

Janet was divorced and had initially moved from teaching children to corporate America for the money. She had two children to raise and a husband who was reluctant to pay child support. She was a good teacher and thrived in this new environment, but with the industry changing, she accepted a buyout and retired for the second time.

She was too young for social security and based on where she was living, her pensions and savings would not cover her living expenses long term. She needed a third career.

We worked together for many months. Our conversations revolved around her new business, getting clients and, more often than not, her grandchildren. She had a grandson and a new granddaughter on the way. Unfortunately, they lived several hours away, but she spent as much time as she could with them.

We decided to accelerate the launch of her workshops series and rented a condo at the shore for a brain-storming and planning weekend. It was winter so the rates were good, and we spent the whole two days designing the launch of her workshop series. We were both excited. She knew her target audience. She was a gifted teacher with an important message. She knew where to find her clients, and she was ready to go.

Again, a large part of the weekend was spent talking about the impending arrival of her granddaughter and the adventures of her four-year-old grandson.

Janet had expressed that her primary values were teaching, empowering others, and creativity. But it was obvious to me that her highest value was family, and it was missing from her list.

As we began to pack up and head home, I asked her, "Janet, if you could live the next ten to twenty years doing anything you wanted, and money wasn't an issue, what would you do?"

She said that was easy, she'd sell her home; pack up; and move south, where it was cheaper to live; and be a grandmother full time.

I asked her if this was a possibility.

She just looked at me and then said, no, she had to have an income.

We parted ways, and over the next few months, she reached out occasionally to update me on her progress, ask for some support, and share her successes. She'd hosted her first workshop and had a few private clients, but she didn't sound happy. When I asked her about it, the conversation always veered back to her missing being a part of her grandchildren's life. She was tired and often exhausted trying to build her business and spend time with the kids, which involved driving five hours or more depending on traffic, one way.

We began to work together again. We focused on self-care and looking at what was most important to her. When Janet and I did the personal life themes and values exercise again, this time she put family and being a grandmother at the top of the list. Teaching, empowering others, and creativity were all still there, but they were now bundled together with family.

Janet had an a-ha moment. Deciding what to do next was an easy decision. The time spent focused on self-care and leaning into what was most important to her gave her the time, space, and energy to act quickly once she knew what she wanted to do.

In a very short period of time, Janet sold her home, at a nice profit, and began renting an inexpensive condo in North Carolina, just miles from her daughter's home. She set her business aside and was enjoying being a full-time grandmother. She said that once she realized that family was her number-one value, with teaching a close second, she said the decision was easy. She got to be a grandmother full time and spend all her days with her family, and although not officially a teacher, she was able to teach and share her life experiences with her grandchildren in some very creative ways.

A few years ago, I heard from her daughter that Janet had died from a very aggressive form of cancer. As I reflected on this sad news, in a way I was happy that

Janet had reevaluated her values and made a choice to be with her family. She may have spent five to ten years working in her own business instead of spending those precious last years being a daily part of her grandchildren's lives.


JOURNAL QUESTIONS AND EXERCISES

### Personal Life Themes and Values Exercise

Personal life themes and values are one of the keys to greater personal awareness. They can also be used to help gain greater clarity and awareness around your dreams and goals, bring your life into alignment and can also be used to craft a personal mission statement.

While doing this exercise you may find that the life themes and values you have identified as the most important are not a priority in your life today. This is an opportunity to reflect on the question "why." Is it because you have chosen a value or belief you think you should choose? Do you need to reprioritize some things in your life so that they play a greater role in your day-to-day living?

Review the list of personal life themes and values that follow and add any that may not be listed.

Begin by circling all those that resonate with you.

From this list identify the ten most important ones; then from this, list your top five and then your top three.

40 SANDY DEMPSEY

You may also identify your number-one personal life theme/value, but this is often difficult.

Usually, your top three answers tend to fluctuate in ranking according to your current life situation, although they will normally remain in the top three.

After you've chosen your top three, put them somewhere you can see them every day.

| | | | |
|---|---|---|---|
| Accountability | Excitement | Job tranquility | Responsibility |
| Achievement | Exercise | Joy | Security |
| Adaptability | Fame | Kindness | Self-expression |
| Advancement and promotion | Family | Knowledge | Self-reliance |
| Adventure | Financial gain | Leadership | Self-respect / self-love |
| Affection (love and caring) | Flexibility | Life-long learning | Serenity |
| Altruism | Forgiveness | Love | Social interaction |
| Arts | Freedom | Loving Kindness | Solitude |
| Assertiveness | Friendships | Loyalty | Solving problems / designing solutions |
| Challenge | Frugality | Marriage | Sophistication |
| Change and variety | Fun | Meaningful work | Spirituality |
| Charity | Generosity | Mentorship | Stability |
| Cleanliness | Gratitude | Money | Status |
| Close relationships | Harmony | Open-mindedness | Supervising others |
| Community | Having a family | Orderliness | Support |
| Competence | Having children | Peace | Sustainability |
| Competition | Helping other people | Personal freedom | Teamwork |
| Cooperation | Helping society | Personal growth and development | Time freedom |
| Courage | Honesty | Physical challenge | Tranquility |
| Creativity | Hope | Physical strength | Truth |
| Dance-movement | Imagination | Pleasure | Uniqueness |
| Decisiveness | Improvement | Power and authority | Volunteering |
| Democracy | Independence | Privacy | Wealth |
| Dependability | Influencing others | Public service | Well-being |
| Ecology & environment & nature | Inner harmony | Quality relationships | Wisdom |
| Economic security | Integrity | Recognition | Work under pressure |
| Effectiveness | Intellectual challenge | Religion | Work with others |
| Excellence | Intellectual status | Reputation | Working alone |

• Based on the exercise given, how are your three highest and most important values reflected in your life today?

• Describe how they make you feel.

• Which themes or values, when expressed, create feelings of wholeness, freedom, peace, harmony, and joy? If you don't feel inspired and motivated by them, are they your family's or social values, instead of your own?

Revisit the list and do the exercise again with this question in mind.

• Explore using your top-three life themes and values to make decisions and choices. Start small; for example, what activities would you like to participate in this weekend? Write about these experiences in your journal.

## TIPS AND SUGGESTIONS

• Do the personal life themes and values exercise with someone you trust. You can use the journal questions previously provided to give each other feedback.

• Keep a decision notebook and jot down what life themes or value played a part in it. Make it fun.

• When a close friend makes a decision, see if they are open to having a conversation to explore what the basis of their decision was and if it was a reflection of their core values and life themes.

# 6

# DELEGATING – THE UNCOMFORTABLE BUT NECESSARY THIRD STEP TO TAKE BACK CONTROL OF YOUR TIME

*"Alone we can do so little; together we can do so much."*

— HELEN KELLER

**M**arilyn looked at me through her Zoom camera. I could feel her frustration. "My life is crazy busy and chaotic. I never have time for me. I'm either working, teaching, taking my mom or dad to the doctor or the grocery store, cooking, cleaning, running the bake sale at church, volunteering at the local women's shelter – ugh – the list is endless. I never have a moment to myself, and no one ever helps me."

No one ever helps her. I've heard that before.

She continued. She was on a roll, and I had to give her space to get it all out. "We have a new project at the office that is going to require some pretty in-depth financial analysis to determine if the project is viable.

The new guy, Bob, has way less on his plate than me, but the CEO asked me to do it, because in his words, 'I trust you, Marilyn, to do it right.' Huh? I thought to myself, well, then, what are you paying Bob for? But I didn't say anything. I did ask Bob to pull some numbers and run a few quick financial models, but he said he was too busy. I didn't push it."

She hardly took a breath as she continued, "At home, once in a while you'd think Joey could cook or bring home dinner. But he thinks it's still 1980 and I'm the woman from the old perfume commercial singing, 'I bring home the bacon, fry it up in a pan and never, never let you forget you are a man.'

"And don't get me started on my brother, who never helps with Mom and Dad. He could take them to the grocery store once in a while, especially when he's not working. He's a union carpenter, and it's slow in the winter. But he always says Mom and Dad want me to take them."

Marilyn visibly collapsed as she repeated, "I never have any help. How will I ever find the time and energy to create the life I want to live?"

Marilyn is like a lot of my clients. They know what they want but are so overwhelmed by their daily life they don't know where to start. They work full time, are married, have elderly parents to care for, do volunteer work, and the list goes on. Marilyn's issue wasn't just that she couldn't say no or hold her boundaries but that she really did need help. She needed to delegate some of what was on her plate to regain some measure of control over her time and energy so she could create the life she wanted before it was too late.

Sharing the load – sharing responsibilities and delegating – is one of the hardest lessons for my clients to implement. They are used to doing it all at home and at work, and they feel guilty if they don't. Part of their identity comes from being a caregiver, for taking care of everyone else, but it comes at a cost. And the cost is that they lose touch with their own dreams, what's important to them, and who they always imagined they would be. It costs them the life they always dreamed of living.

## SHARING THE LOAD AND DELEGATING

Sharing the load and delegating responsibilities has been one of the hardest lessons for me to learn. But by learning to delegate my life flows so much more easily. I'm happier. I have more time to be creative. I have more time for fun activities and experiences. I get to do the things I love and that I'm good at. I have more time for self-care, friends, and family. And I'm more productive.

One of the reasons why it is so hard to ask others for help is that it can feel really good when we are the ones doing everything. We get compliments about how much we do, and we feel good about getting so much done. We also burn out and have no time for other activities or other people.

I know personally that having a long to-do list

where I can check things off gives me a sense of satisfaction and accomplishment. The problem is when my to-do list is the only thing giving me this feeling and when this feeling becomes more important than anything else.

I'm lucky in one way: I have a pretty high energy level and love to solve problems. Now, at the same time, because of this capacity I can also ignore when I'm tired, get caught up doing things, and forget about *being* – paying attention to the moment, what is happening, what I'm feeling and thinking, and who I'm with. I also can burn out quickly and lose all my energy and enthusiasm.

When I first became a manager decades ago, the position came with a lot of responsibility – not just my own, but that of my whole department. I thought I could do it all. At first, I loved the challenge and dove right in, but after months of doing nothing but work, at the office and at home, it became too much; I wanted to quit.

It was easier for me to do everything than to document what needed to be done and then delegate and teach someone else. Writing things down was tedious, and I hated tedium. Plus, when I did something, like create a report, I was always looking at how I could tweak it, make it better, automate the process, and so on. How could I teach that to someone else?

One day I sat down and made a list of everything that needed to get done on a daily, weekly, monthly, and annual basis. Everything. Then I listed who was responsible for each item. Of course, my name was on way more items than there was time for in a day, and there were a whole lot of things on the list that I hated doing and items that pulled me away from the more important tasks. For example, for me to track the weekly productivity rates by doing all the data entry was a poor use of my time. I needed to focus on analyzing the data, making sure the report was correct, or doing something else, like writing the budget.

After I made the list, I had to identify who I could delegate tasks to and when I'd train them. This took some time. Sometimes, I'd write the instructions and document the process. Then I decided to delegate that, too.

## ASK, DON'T TELL

When I first approached my assistant I asked, "What do you think about helping me document how we create the weekly production report and then taking it over each week?"

I was asking because I personally hated it when someone directly told me what to do, so I didn't want to be that kind of boss. Just as I wanted to feel like I had some say in the matter, I wanted my employees to feel the same way. By asking instead of telling, I was also able to track how engaged each employee was in their job and in the company and get a feel for if they were just showing up to do the minimum and collect a paycheck or if they wanted to grow and learn with the company.

By asking instead of telling, my employees also felt their opinions and ideas counted. It also told them that I respected them and that I needed them.

When we started, I said, "This is super important, and because I want you to really understand how this process works, I'm going to have you write the notes yourself as we go along. Next week, I'll have you train Jackie using your notes, and then you can add anything we may have missed. Then we'll review it together."

I was empowering my assistant to take control of her position and by having her train someone else she knew. This way, whenever she was off, the work would still get done, and she knew that not everything was on her shoulders. I did not want my staff to fall into the same patterns I had, thinking they had to do everything and that they were the only one that could do it right.

This process wasn't easy. I still fell back into my old bad habits sometimes of thinking I had to do it all. But over time it did become easier. And as we moved forward, we were the only department that had the most detailed standard operating procedures (SOP).

Every company has turnover, and by having this training manual, it was so easy to onboard new employees and get them up to speed quickly. It also gave the new employee a boost of confidence.

## DELEGATING: THE BENEFITS

The surprising thing about learning to delegate was that I was able to keep learning new things instead of getting bogged down in the day-to-day "doing." Because I get bored easily and have an insatiable desire to learn more, I was continually able to take on new projects and responsibilities. As I was promoted, I was able to promote and bring up the people who worked for me.

As a consultant on the side, beginning to document the processes a company had was one of the first things I usually looked at and put into action. Most of the companies I've worked for over the years either as an employee or as a consultant were relatively new companies that grew very quickly. Most of the managers and owners were just like me, they were used to doing everything that needed to be done on their own and had very little if any of their processes documented.

My consulting clients were very similar to my current coaching clients. They started out knowing what they wanted, began to bring their ideas and dreams to life and ended up spending all their time and energy doing everything but living the life they dreamed of. They had to learn the same things I learned and teach my clients now – to share the load and delegate so they could have the time, energy, and freedom to create a full life, not just professionally, but personally as well

When I finally had a well-trained staff and an SOP manual, my work life became so much more exciting and less stressful. I also discovered how much I enjoyed working with people, training them, teaching them skills that once they mastered no one could take away from them, mentoring them as they grew, and encouraging them to do the things they loved both at work and at home. This was the beginning of my coaching career.

There is power in asking for help and sharing the load. Suddenly, so many more things are possible; new doors open, and everyone wins.

## OUTSOURCING AND HIRING HELP

In my own businesses – and I've had many, most often as a side hustle – I learned to budget hiring help as soon as I could afford it. Because my time was so limited, sharing the load and delegating was a must if I wanted to maximize the use of it.

For example, early on I taught myself HTML and built my own websites from scratch. I then progressed to easier platforms like WordPress and learned more coding so I could customize the websites. I really loved it because I was constantly learning something new, solving problems, and figuring things out. But that wasn't my business. And, the more time I spent customizing the website, the graphics, the apps and widgets, as fun as it was, the less time I was spending on finding clients and working directly with them.

As soon as I could afford it, I invested and hired a graphic artist to create a new logo and graphics for me. It was my concept and looked way better than anything

I could have created on my own. They were the professionals; I was not. Instead of spending hours and hours learning how to use graphic design software and then more hours trying to get my logo and images just right, I delegated this work and hired someone who did it for a living. They could give me what I wanted in one-tenth the amount of time it would take me to do it, and they could give me exactly what I wanted; plus, it looked professional versus amateurish.

The time and money I spent on buying software, teaching myself, and doing the work was way more than just researching the best graphic artist I could afford to ask them for what I wanted.

## THE HOME FRONT

Applying the concept of sharing the load at home is important, too, because our life isn't just about work. For me, there are things I hate to do, like mow the grass. Sharing the household responsibilities or hiring someone to do what I dislike frees me up to do the things I do enjoy, or frees up my time for self-care, for spending time with people I love and care about, and to just relax.

I remember the first time I came home from work and pulled in the driveway after the lawn service had left. I just sat and stared at my beautiful yard. The grass was mowed. The bushes were all trimmed. The ivy was under control. The roses were blooming. It was gorgeous and I hadn't had to lift a finger break a sweat to make it happen. It was such a powerful moment. Now I could come home, get a glass of iced tea, a book, and my journal and sit on the back porch admiring my beautiful yard, reading and relaxing instead of putting on my work clothes; dragging the mower out of the garage; finding the gas can; spending hours mowing, clipping, and trimming; then putting everything way; taking a shower; and collapsing on the couch, too tired to read.

Sharing the load and delegating had been one of the biggest turning points in my personal and professional life and one of the biggest factors in being able to do more of what I love and create the life I love. I shared this with Marilyn, the client you met at the beginning of this chapter.

I had Marilyn go back over the time bank she'd created when we were reviewing her self-care needs (Chapter 4) and identify one activity she disliked doing and that she could delegate or hire someone to do for her. Cooking was her answer. She disliked shopping and preparing meals, although she loved good food, as did her husband. I asked her how she thought she could delegate these activities. Asking her husband, Joey, to take it over wasn't an option. First, he wasn't a good cook, and second, he was just as busy as she was.

We continued to brainstorm ideas, and she decided to look into how much it would cost to hire a personal chef to shop and prepare five dinners a week for her and her husband. She was surprised that it wasn't as expensive as she'd originally thought. She and Joey talked about it, and they both agreed to give it a try.

Marilyn reported back to me that the personal chef idea had not only given her several hours back a week, but she felt better and was less stressed because she was eating better and wasn't running around shopping and cooking. The idea was such a success she hired the same chef to shop and prepare meals for her parents, who were delighted. Now, Marilyn got to spend quality, relaxed time with her parents sharing a meal.

Marilyn was hooked on delegating, and we began working together so she could share even more of her load. She felt in control of her time and her life again. She now had the time to begin exploring the dreams she'd put on the back burner years ago and envision a new, more meaningful life, that she could begin creating now instead of some faraway time in the future.

JOURNAL QUESTIONS AND EXERCISES

• Revisit your time bank that you completed in Chapter 4 to help determine what activities and responsibilities you should continue to do and which ones you should delegate:

○ Highlight the activities you enjoy doing in green and highlight the tasks and activities you dislike in pink.

○ Which of these items could you delegate to someone else or hire someone else to do for you?
○ Pick one item you can delegate this week to someone else.

• Was this an easy or difficult step for you? Why?

• How is regaining control of your time by sharing the load and delegating beginning to change your life? What are you feeling? Thinking? Dreaming about?

• Pick someone famous whom you admire and make a list of everything you think they delegate to someone else in their life. How could you model this behavior?

• For fun, imagine delegating everything in your life and doing only the things you absolutely love to do. Explore this in your journal with words and pictures (draw or clip pictures from the internet (digital journal) or magazines (pen and paper journal).

TIPS AND SUGGESTIONS

• When preparing to delegate a task, think about how you can ask for assistance versus assigning a task or activity to someone else.

• Begin documenting, or assign someone to document, what needs to be done, when it needs to be done, and the important steps needed to be taken to complete a given task or activity.

• If you are doing this at home and your kids are old enough, invite them to participate and help you – and even take over some of the household tasks that need to be done.

# 7

# SUPPORT – THE MUST-HAVE FOURTH STEP TO TAKING BACK CONTROL OF YOUR TIME

*"God, grant me the serenity to accept the things I cannot change, courage to change the things I can, and wisdom to know the difference."*

— SERENITY PRAYER

Receiving support is hard for many people because it goes way beyond delegating and hiring others to do the things you don't want to do or don't like to do.

Support is more of a surrender. It's not asking someone to *do* something for you, it's more about asking others to *be* there for you. Oftentimes, yes, they will do things for you as well, but it's primarily about allowing others to be with you in both the good times and bad.

When Jocelyn came to me, she had what others considered a good job working for the city government, but she hated it. She dreaded going in on Mondays. She disliked the political jockeying and squabbles and the job itself bored her to tears. She only worked forty hours a week, but she felt like they were wasted hours and that she'd never get to do the things she wanted to do.

When I asked her to tell me about what she wanted, she sat up straight, looked me in the eye and leaned forward. "I want to lead painting retreats for women survivors of breast cancer and those in treatment. I want to take them to the beach where they can feel the sun and the air and smell the ocean. I want them to experience the healing power of paint on canvas even if they've never painted before."

She was so passionate about what she wanted. She studied art in college but had never followed through with it until she'd picked up a paintbrush again following her cancer diagnosis.

When I asked what was stopping her from making her dream come true, her shoulders slumped again. "My job is so draining. It's boring. And when I get home all I do is run around taking care of my brother, who's disabled; taking care of my parents, who are now in their eighties; and doing the books for my husband's lawn care business."

I gave her a few minutes, and she continued, "When I was going through treatments, I took time off from work. I started going to therapy. Friends and family stepped in to help my brother and parents. My husband was so great. There were days all I did was cry, and he was right there for me. He even hired a part-time book-keeper. It felt like, for the first time in my life, I was able to relax, let others do things for me instead of the other way around and just be there for me. I had time to paint, read, and dream. But as soon as the treatments were finished and I went back to work, it didn't take long for everything to go back to the way they were before. Now, I have no time and no energy to do what I want."

Jocelyn had surrendered once. She'd realized that she couldn't do everything on our own. She recognized that she needed support, kind words, safe space, respite, celebration, counsel.

## KNOWING WHAT KIND OF SUPPORT YOU NEED

Learning to surrender and receive support has been a hard one for me, too. It's not even in my nature to think about asking for support. I just assume that whatever needs to be done, I can do it or figure out how to do it. It's always been about doing something, the action, and not about the being.

But in 2007, when my mom was diagnosed with breast cancer for the second time, now metastasized, it brought me to my knees. I'd already lost my father to esophageal cancer twelve years prior. My mom already battled breast cancer once, with complications from chemo, blood clots, and having to have her kidney removed. Now this.

I've always shouldered whatever came down the pike, willing to do whatever was needed and support those around me. However, asking for help and support for myself wasn't in my vernacular. I was the classic overachiever and overgiver, always taking care of everyone else at my own expense. How could I stop now, when Mom needed me the most? I couldn't stop, but I knew I couldn't do it alone either this time. I needed help. I needed support. I needed more than just someone to delegate the grocery shopping to or to take Mom to the doctors. I had to let go and surrender to the fact that I couldn't be the only person to provide the physical, emotional, spiritual, intellectual, and financial support for her.

Asking for support wasn't easy. My therapist was my first line of support; then my friends provided a second layer, a place for me to just "be" with my sadness, anger and grief. Seeking this type of support was new for me and was really difficult. In our family we were raised to keep family stuff within the circle of family and not invite in the outside world. We handled our own stuff, and we certainly didn't share personal information with anyone, sometimes not even within the family. I broke that rule.

When my mom was diagnosed, I was working a full-time day job and following my dreams of writing, teaching, and building a business as a side hustle.

Like many of my clients, I had a lot on my plate, and I didn't know how I was going to be able to do it all.

I had to step back. And just like when my clients or

employees would get overwhelmed, I asked some basic questions. What was most important to me? What types of support did both my mom and I need? What could I ask others to do so I didn't have as much on my plate? What did I need to let go of? I began to slow down and look around me.

My mom was important to me. I didn't want her to suffer and that was important to me.

My husband was important to me. Our time together was very important to me.

Continuing to write, teach, and build my business was important to me.

And continuing to earn a living, pay my bills, and support my mom financially was important to me.

Those were my priorities.

In terms of support, it started with the most basic of support, asking for help doing things.

I needed help taking my mom to and from doctor appointments. My sister, despite working full-time and having three small children, was willing to take Mom to some of her treatments.

I talked to my boss about taking extra time off, so instead of rushing around getting done what had to get done, I had time to slow down and just sit with my mom, watch TV together, go to lunch, and visit friends and family.

I also surrendered by sharing publicly what was happening. I'd built a small audience through my side business, and I decided to write about and share what was happening with them. I was nervous. I had to let go of the image that I had it all together. Sharing publicly broke every rule we had growing up, but these people had been reading my blogs and receiving my newsletter for years, and I felt close to them. I'd also met many of them in the classes I taught or at events we attended together. As a teacher, I felt it was important that they knew that my life wasn't perfect and, like them, I struggled.

There was an outpouring of offers for prayers and kind words of support. It felt very comforting. Many people shared similar stories from their own lives, and we bonded even more deeply. They weren't doing anything in the sense of taking things off my plate, but their support was just as important because I knew others cared, they understood, and many had been in my shoes, so I felt less alone. This helped make my situation easier for me to navigate.

## SUPPORT BEYOND A CRISIS

Both Jocelyn and I had experienced what it was like to have support during a crisis. What would it be like to have support the rest of the time?

For me, I continued to open to receiving support. I became more authentic in my sharing on social media and in my writing. Friendships became deeper and more about giving and receiving. Some friendships fell away, but those that remained became stronger as we shared more and supported one another. It's an amazing feeling to know that you can just share with another how you feel and what you are thinking and just have them hold space for you without trying to do anything or fix it for you.

I wanted this same thing for Jocelyn. We tackled self-care, using her values and personal life themes to make decisions, and delegating first. She began to feel more in control of her time and excited by the possibilities of bringing to fruition her dreams of leading painting retreats for women with breast cancer. So, we then, as our next step, began to look at what she needed for support.

Jocelyn had me on her support team. Who else did she need?

She decided she needed to be around other artists. When we talked about it, she realized that it wasn't just artists she wanted to be with, but those who supported themselves with their art and teaching about their art. First, she began to take classes with those she admired and then began to naturally develop relationships with the classmates she resonated with and some of the instructors. She began to feel seen, and her ideas of leading painting retreats were accepted and cheered her on.

Jocelyn also discovered that not everyone will say yes when you ask for support. There will be some people who will say no when you reach out or, sometimes, criticize you, which is the opposite of what you need. She found this out when one of her oldest friends started telling her that her ideas wouldn't work and picking them apart. Whenever we met and she reported this to me, she cried. She was hurt and angry. She eventually stopped talking to this friend about her dreams and ideas, and her friend slowly drifted away. They occasionally saw each other when they met with mutual friends, but the closeness wasn't there anymore. At first, this bothered Jocelyn, but when we talked about it and she recognized that she needed people in her life who lifted her up, she was able to let go of this old friendship. When she did, she was surprised that new relationships that were more mutually supportive filled the gap.

Even at home, she found the support she needed. Her relationship with her husband had deepened when she was going through treatments, but when things slipped back into the old patterns when she went back to work, she never said anything and never shared how unhappy she was. Once she began to talk with her husband and tell him about the dream she had of leading painting retreats for women with breast cancer, she was surprised and delighted by his enthusiasm for the idea. He told her he'd support her in any way that she wanted him to. He loved her, wanted her to be happy, and wanted them to live a long life together. He, too, had a secret longing that he shared with her, giving her the chance to support him, and their relationship grew even deeper.

JOURNAL QUESTIONS AND EXERCISES

• To reclaim your dreams, what support do you need?

• What does it look like for you? Feel like?

• Who in your life can feel these roles?

• What other types of support do you need?

• Where could you find it?

• Who or what do you need to let go of to make room for support in your life?

• What's stopping you from receiving the support you want and need?

TIPS AND SUGGESTIONS

• Ask for the support you need.

• Don't expect everyone to be able to support you or your dreams or to fill every supportive role you need.

• Don't take on another's fears, criticism, or judgments.

• Be kind to others; they too may have buried dreams that were never supported.

• Be willing to let go of relationships that aren't mutually supportive.

• Invite new friendships into your life and take the time to nurture them.

• Invest in yourself by hiring and working with a life coach, healers like energy workers and massage therapists, taking classes, attending workshops, or working with a therapist or counselor if there are deeper issues you need to work through.

8

---

# KEY #1 – VISUALIZE THE
# DETAILS

*"In order to manifest our destiny in the world, we first have to create it within."*

— DAN MILLMAN

W hat's your life purpose? Your *big* dream? You know it. You've been carrying it around in your back pocket for years, maybe even decades. Every once in a while, you take it out and dreamily stare at it.

You know the dreams you left behind. You are ready to take them back. If you weren't ready, you wouldn't be reading this book.

I used to be you. I had a *big* dream. It felt like more than a dream. It felt like a calling, a purpose.

I love to write and teach. I love business. I love to use my creativity to solve real world problems and to help others. I love the journey, the process of moving forward toward a target.

Although I cannot control the result or the outcome, I want people to feel seen and heard in my presence. I want them to be supported, to have confidence that they can move forward and to have tools that they can use to live their life purpose and create a life they love by combining all their gifts, talents, interests, ideas and experiences. I want them to walk away feeling inspired and to take action.

I've defined my life purpose as helping alleviate suffering – my own and others'. The *big* dream is to inspire, empower, and support others to live a life of purpose and meaning. I do this through creativity expressed in my own business – writing, teaching, coaching, and hands-on healing. It is what I've been called to do for decades. My values of personal growth and learning, creativity, and embodying loving kindness are built into my work and guide me when making decisions.

In this chapter, we are going to take back your dreams now that you have regained control of your time and begin exploring the six keys to an effective action plan. These aren't step by step instructions that you will take one at a time, although you may start out doing just that. These are keys that you will use over and over again and circle back to when you are in the midst of creating and living the life you want. So, what are they?

• Key #1: Visualize the Details – we will begin to visualize the details of the life you want and begin fleshing out the details to your dreams.

• Key #2: Determine the Right Time – we'll take your dream, and the details you envisioned for the life you want and look to see if it's the right time and the right place, and what you may need to change, let go of or expand.

• Key #3: Set Your Targets – we will explore the difference between goals and targets and we will make sure your targets are meaningful to you, measurable, achievable, and exciting.

• Key #4: Break It Down – we get down to the nitty gritty here and start to create your plan of action by breaking things down into small steps.

• Key #5: Plan for Missteps – we'll look at what happens when things don't go right, when we fall down and take missteps.

• Key #6: Dream Bigger – in our final step to creating an effective action plan, we'll explore what it's like to expand your vision even more so that your dreams keep growing and you can continue living the life you want.

## FLESHING OUT THE DETAILS

When I started working with Rita, introduced in Chapter 1, she had an idea for an event planning business. She loved organizing events, connecting people and helping people celebrate the important moments in their lives. But beyond that, she wasn't sure what it looked like.

Just like we did in earlier chapters, we looked at her values which were celebration, creativity, and community. We looked at what she loved, which was thinking through all the details, big and small, that would make an event successful. She was extremely detail-oriented and loved making lists and notes. She was highly creative and had an eye for color, style, and aesthetics. She loved taking a client's idea and making it come alive in a way the client may not have imagined. Rita was also good at managing others because she really appreciated what they did and who they were. To me, it looked like herding cats, everyone running around in a gazillion directions, but she always knew where everyone should be and what they should be doing. She reminded me of Jennifer Lopez's character in *The Wedding Planner*.

However, she needed to both focus and flesh out her dream at the same time. Who was she going to serve? What types of events were the best fit for her gifts, talents, and interests? How did the events she wanted to produce align with her values?

First, Rita had to decide if she wanted to work with corporate clients or individuals. When she looked at her values and her experience, she realized that working with corporate clients would put limits around her creativity as they typically had very strict guidelines about what they wanted. She wanted to create events that were celebrations of a more personal nature than promoting the launch of a new product, which had been her experience in the past.

Now she knew she wanted to work with individuals. She knew the events would be some type of personal celebration, but what? Weddings? Births? Life celebrations? Anniversaries? All of the above?

We stepped back a bit, and I had Rita start to take time every day to visualize and allow her imagination to run wild and begin to project herself into the future as an event planner. I asked her to do this for a week and record in her journal her experiences, not just the details, but how she felt.

When we met, Rita was super excited. She kept seeing a barn at different times of the year, decorated in different ways. A barn? I couldn't see it, but Rita did, which is all that mattered. She went on to describe these beautiful fundraising events for different organizations. Fundraising? She'd never mentioned this before. Rita herself was surprised. Still, when we talked, it made perfect sense. She had always been involved in the community and supported several causes and volunteered several times a year at the animal shelter and food bank.

Now her dream was starting to feel more real. It had some texture to it.

When I asked her about the barn, she said there was a piece of property she and her husband had looked at many times over the past few years and had considered buying. The property had a small home, several acres and a very large barn on it. Every time she'd driven past it, she imagined the yard and barn bright with lights, music, and laughter. She wasn't sure if they'd buy the property or if it was just a part of the imagery that helped her envision her dream, but she held it as a possibility for the future.

My concern, but not Rita's, was how she would get paid for a fundraiser for a nonprofit. Her target wasn't to get rich, as she was sure she'd earn the money she needed for her current lifestyle and enough to save for retirement. She knew her events would be hugely successful and that was worth something. Most nonprofit leaders had so much on their plate, and despite the importance of fundraising, it often fell to the wayside until push came to shove and funds were running low. Rita was sure that she could create a calendar of events, large and small, for several of the local nonprofit organizations in a way that they could have continuous funding. It was a win-win. She'd be doing what she loved, supporting causes she believed in. The events would support the community as she'd use local businesses for them and the larger community would benefit from the services the nonprofits would provide.

I encouraged Rita to speak to some of the local leaders she knew to see if her idea was valid. She came and reported that it was. Rita knew the direction she wanted to go in.

I understood where Rita was coming from, as I'd been in the place many times. She had no guarantees, but she now had some meat around her idea, a place to start, and a vision as to where she wanted to go.

## LET YOUR IDEA GROW

There are no guarantees in life and even less when you decide to follow your heart and listen to your soul's call. Very few people step outside the norm and build a life purposefully. It takes courage and perseverance. It's easier when you are doing it with a solid foundation under your feet, aware of your values and your why.

When I first started the Dreaming Café, most of my family and friends could not understand why I'd spend all my free time building a business when I already had a well-paying job that I liked and that took up a lot of my time. What they didn't understand was that the Dreaming Café gave meaning to my life. It was based on what was most important to me, it was an outlet for my creativity, and it gave me an opportunity to reach more people and make a difference in the world. It started as a small idea, just a blog. Then it expanded to teaching and leading my own events. When a reader or client would send me a message or stop me after a live event and tell me how much my work, my words, had impacted their lives, those were the moments that made it all worthwhile.

I'd have never reached that point if I hadn't spent time imagining and visualizing what my idea could look like, feel like, and grow into.

My current business would have never been born if I hadn't followed that first idea through all those years ago. I would have never taken the step and committed to write this book if I hadn't taken the initial idea for the Dreaming Café and allowed it to grow.

It starts with an idea, grounded in your values, gifts, talents, interests, and experiences and grows from there. You start to flesh out the idea, move forward, take action one step and a time and sometimes the original idea grows bigger than you could have imagined.

But, it takes one step at a time and the first step is to take the seed of your idea and begin adding the details to make it real. That's what I did, what Rita did, what my clients do and what I want you to do. No one can have the same positive impact on the world as you can. You deserve it to yourself and the world to dig deep, flesh out your dream, give it some substance and then start building that dream.

## JOURNAL QUESTIONS AND EXERCISES

### *Visualization Exercise*

Find a quiet spot where you can sit quietly for fifteen minutes. Have your journal with you, a pen and some colored markers, pencils, or crayons. If it's still hard for you to find a few quiet moments alone, try this exercise in the car before starting your day or before going into the house at the end of the day.

Now close your eyes. Take a deep breath through your nose, counting to three slowly, breathing all the way down into your belly, feel it expand, hold, count to three, and slowly to the count of three release your breath through your mouth feeling your belly sink toward your spine.

Allow your mind to empty while you take four more breaths. Now, on the next inhale, feel your body relax, return to a slow, normal breath.

With your eyes still closed, breathing slowly, imagine yourself in an empty room. The room is white, soft, and almost feels like you are floating in a cloud. You are relaxed and at ease. People begin to enter the room. Chairs appear for them to sit in. These are all people you respect, admire, and feel comfortable with.

Butterflies dance in your stomach in a good way. You begin to feel excited. You are standing in front of the room, and everyone is now looking at you, waiting for you to speak. They have all shown up to hear you speak about how you brought your dream to life. They are here for you to share your success story with them.

Imagine yourself looking at each of the people in the room one at a time. Feel their love and support. Lean into it. Draw courage from it.

Now, slowly begin to describe your dream. Leave nothing out. No detail is too small or too big. Feel their enthusiasm grow as yours does. Share more. Where did your dream originate? How long has it lived in your heart? What were your first steps? What obstacles did you face and how did you overcome them? How has bringing your dream to reality changed your life? Changed others?

As you talk, your dream grows bigger, the details more specific.

When you are finished, everyone rushes forward to shake your hand or to embrace you. You did it. You took back control of your time and life, reclaimed your dreams and took action to create the life you wanted. Now your story is inspiring others.

As the room empties and people leave, you feel a sense of peace and satisfaction. You are on the right track. You are living your dreams. Your life has meaning and purpose. You've created the life you always dreamed of.

Now slowly take a deep breath through your nose, counting to three slowly, breathing all the way down into your belly, feel it expand, hold, count to three, and slowly, to the count of three, release your breath through your mouth feeling your belly sink toward your spine.

Allow your mind to empty while you take four more breaths. Now, on the next inhale, feel your body relax, return to a slow, normal breath, and open your eyes.

JOURNAL QUESTIONS

In your journal, with words and/or pictures explore the following questions:

• What surprised you when sharing about living your dream and the life you always imagined?

• What obstacles did you face?

• How did you overcome them?

• Who supported your dreams and what role did they play?

• What inspired you about your vision?

• What difference were you making in your life and the lives of others?

• What steps did you take to achieve your dream and create the life you described?

TIPS AND SUGGESTIONS

• Do this visualization exercise several days in a row and look at how the details change.

• Explore the different scenarios your imagination brings forth.

• Play with how you can capture the details and essence of your vision:

    ○ Write in your journal.
    ○ Draw a picture or a series of pictures.
    ○ Make a vision board.
    ○ Create a PowerPoint presentation.
    ○ Play with Legos.
    ○ Make a diorama (a replica of a scene, typically a three-dimensional full-size or miniature model.)

# 9

# KEY #2 – DETERMINE THE RIGHT TIME

*"If we want to live fully, beyond the life we have today, we must take risks, stretch ourselves, move past what we are now."*

— MARSHA SINETAR

You have some tools in your tool belt to take back control of your life and have time and energy now to devote to what you want. In the last chapter, you visualized and fleshed out your dream, put a little more meat around the vision and began to see and feel what it could look like.

In this next step, we are going dig a little deeper into the details of your dream.

You might be asking yourself, "What does this mean? Didn't we just do that in the last chapter?"

Kind of, but not exactly.

Now we are going to take the vision and the details

and make it even more specific. We're going to look to see whether it's the right time and the right place. You can have a really big dream for which not every piece can happen at the same time. In this step, we are going to look at where you are now and see how close you are to your big dreams, what you may need to change, let go of, or expand on. You are going to reevaluate your vision and revisit your dreams in a way that will allow you to determine where to focus.

We'll dive more into action steps in a later chapter, but before you can do that you have to decide what part of your dream you are going to focus on right now, in this moment. You have the BIG vision and you've visualized the details; now it's time to figure out where to start.

I reevaluate and revisit my big dreams every year, usually in the fall as my birthday approaches. Some people do this around New Year's when they are setting their goals and resolutions. You can do it when you first decide to make your dreams a reality and then pick an annual timeframe in which to revisit your dreams.

For me, this exercise always helps me gauge how close I am to my *best* life and what I want to change, add, and take away.

For instance, writing and publishing a book has been on my to-do list and vision board for many years, but it's not always been a priority until this past year. It also didn't have a purpose. Just saying I wanted to write a book was one thing. Stating that I wanted to write a nonfiction book to share my ideas and methods to help women reclaim their dreams, take back control of their time, and create an action plan to make it happen was a whole different thing. I also knew my own life was changing, I had more time, and I wanted to make a bigger impact. I knew I could reach more people with a book than just in my private practice. As my birthday approached in 2022, I realized that it was now time to make this part of my big dream happen.

## BIG DREAMS: FOCUSING ON ONE DETAIL AT A TIME AND NEVER GIVING UP

In 2022, I recognized that I'd created a lot of the things I envisioned for my life and fulfilled a lot of dreams.

I asked myself, "What's shifted in my world? Why was this year different? What details stood out in my vision?"

I was living in a part of the country I'd always dreamed of. My husband and I had traveled most of the central and western parts of the country. I was preparing for my final year of my four-year studies with the Barbara Brennan School of Healing. I was slowly building my part-time private practice into a full-time practice. And, I'd achieved the professional success I'd worked for many years, so many things were coming to a close, creating space for something new.

For example, in my role as COO/CFO of the company I helped manage, I finally had my dream team. I knew I'd be transitioning out of this position and away from the company, so having a strong team in place was essential. Since I started working for this company, I'd always envisioned a group of skilled and motivated women, moms to be exact, bilingual, working twenty-five to forty hours a week each, cross-trained to cover for each other, and able to work independently. And, that's exactly what I was able to manifest. They were awesome and the best support team I've ever had!

This support and knowing that within eighteen to twenty-four months this position would be coming to a close was creating space for something new.

That something new was finding space to allow me to grow my private practice.

In 2019, I'd tried to expand on my dream and found a coleasing space about twenty minutes from my home. I signed the lease the day the governor shut the state down due to the pandemic. After a year of paying for the space and only using it occasionally, I let the lease go in 2020. It just wasn't the right time, and I had to let that part of my dream go.

I didn't let everything about my dream go. I had a great home office out of which I could do all my online client work, but it isn't the dream space I've always envisioned.

Since I moved to Washington State, I'd always wanted my own office within a few miles of my home for my private coaching and healing practice. I kept looking, but for the first six years I lived here, I couldn't find anything.

In 2022, as my birthday approached, I once again felt called to find an office close to home and held that vision in my mind. I wanted to grow my private practice, and I wanted to see more in-person clients from my community. To do this, I needed a physical space in which to grow my business. I felt like one door was closing (my day job) and a new door was opening (a full-time private practice).

One day, out of the blue, we were driving home from the grocery store when my husband spotted an "office for lease" sign from the highway. I was so excited. Was this it? I immediately called when I got home and left a message. The next day, I drove past and tried to peak in the windows. I couldn't see how big it was, but it was in a small building, with two massage therapists, a veterinarian clinic, and a specialty kitchen store. It was less than three miles from my house, in a great location, easy to find, and had lots of parking. I wanted this office. I called again and left another message. This went on for a few weeks, and I was ready to give up. I decided to try one more time, and decided to use my Washington cell phone instead of my personal cell phone that had a Jersey area code.

The owner answered right away. We talked a bit about what I did. He wanted to make sure I wasn't going to be competition for the existing tenants, told me the rent (a little more than I wanted to pay but reasonable), and explained that it was four hundred square feet. He said I could have it. I was over the moon and asked to see the inside before I said yes. The space was cluttered when I met the property manager as the previous tenants hadn't moved out yet, but the office was way bigger than I thought; I could immediately see myself working there. In a matter of days, I signed the lease, and the space was mine. It was big enough to not only work one-on-one with clients but also teach classes or lead groups of nine to twelve people. I was so excited. The vision I'd held for six years was finally becoming a reality.

Now, the next piece was to really feel into what I wanted the space to look like. I'd already created an office in the cocreating space in 2019, and I'd had a home office in both New Jersey and Washington. So, I knew what I liked, disliked, and needed. I knew I needed to create a space that was minimalistic, with wood and steel accents and lots of light. I spent hours online looking at furniture. I then did a scale drawing of what I wanted with the furniture I picked out. Then I used painters' tape on the floor to lay out the imagined furniture. Knowing what would fit and what wouldn't, I ordered what I needed. In the end, the office came together just as I'd imagined and felt so good. I can work in that space for hours and time stands still. The clients I see in person are comfortable and at ease. I use the office for my online clients and to write. It's a dream come true.

## SEEING THE DETAILS AND FOCUSING

When Janet, whom you met in Chapter 5, and I explored the questions, "What has shifted in your world? Why was this year different? What details stand out in your vision?" In our getaway weekend, she always "saw" big open spaces with lots of trees and with her grandkids always around. Trees and big open spaces didn't really reflect the highly industrialized urban area she was living in, and her grandkids didn't live close by. It was one of the keys that made me ask her about what she really wanted to create. And, as you know, although her life purpose was about teaching, it was about doing that more in the context of being a grandmother than as a workshop leader.

When I walked Patrice, another client, through these questions, her *best* life looked and felt like a party, like a huge celebration. The environment she saw herself in was like a giant dance floor. When she imagined how her days looked, she saw herself making breakfast for her kids before driving them to school, talking on the phone in her own office, creating designs on the computer in the afternoon, going to after-school soccer games and dance rehearsals and attending parties some evenings and weekends. They were parties she organized and hosted for birthdays, wedding anniversaries, graduations, and other big family moments. Patrice was the second event planner I worked with, although she called herself a party planner, and her vision was very different than Rita's. Her clients were different and she saw herself not only owning an event space in an urban area but also creating a business that included her whole family.

Patrice began by focusing on one aspect of her BIG dream at a time. First, she rented spaces as she needed them and hired her family to help her. She took one step at a time and over time, Patrice leased and then purchased a hall that she could rent out for parties, in addition to organizing the parties. She was an in-demand party planner and handled everything in house. She'd created a kind of co-op with other family members for furniture rental, decorations, and catering. Family was one of her top values, and it was expressed multidimensionally in her life and her business.

Patrice was able to see her big dream but, based on where she was in her life, focused on one aspect of her vision at a time until she eventually created the exact life she'd envisioned.

## JOURNAL QUESTIONS AND EXERCISES

• What is different in your life now or what is ending to create space for something new?

• Imagine your very *best* life.

  ○ What does it look like, feel like?
  ○ What environment are you working and thriving in?
  ○ What are you doing on a daily, weekly, or monthly basis?
  ○ How are you living your life?
  ○ What are you wearing?
  ○ Who are you interacting with?

• What aspects of your vision feel doable now and which ones feel like it might not be the right time? Why or why not?

• Describe a situation in the past that you tried to make happen, but it wasn't the right time. How did you handle it?

TIPS AND SUGGESTIONS

• Be as specific as possible when envisioning your dream. Colors. Textures. Sounds.

• Don't put any limits on the details when describing your very BEST life.

• Read a biography or autobiography of someone you admire. Where in their life did they let go of something to create space for something new? How specific were they in envisioning the life they wanted to create?

## KEY #3 – SET YOUR TARGETS

*"Doing the work you love requires that you be equally comfortable with the imaginative and the practical. It requires the ability to dream big dreams and the ability to confront and master all the little details that go into making dreams come true."*

— LAURENCE G. BOLDT

What is the difference between goals and targets? First, let's look at a few definitions:

*Goal:* "the end toward which effort is directed" (www.Merriam-Webster.com); "the object of a person's ambition or effort; an aim or desired result" (www. Google.com) "something that you are trying to do or achieve" (www.Britannica.com)

*Target:* "a mark to shoot at; a goal to be achieved" (www.Merriam-Webster.com); "a person, object, or

place selected as the aim of an attack" (www.
Google.com); "something that you are trying to do or
achieve" (www.Britannica.com)

Basically, goals are fixed points, and you either meet
your goal or you don't. When you hit your goal it's like
that three-point shot just as the buzzer sounds. It's an
adrenaline rush and an all-out celebration. When you
miss the shot, the whole world feels like it just came
down around you. Goals are very black and white. You
can swing from one end of the spectrum to the other
with no middle ground.

On the other hand, targets are made to be aimed for,
but there's a little wiggle room. A bull's-eye is awesome,
but if you land outside the bull's-eyes, it is still good and
shows you how far from the center you are. It's a place
to step back and see how close or how far away you are.
There is still a place for celebration, but it's not black
and white, success or failure.

The idea of setting targets versus goals isn't new,
and it's not my idea. I read about it or heard about it
years ago. I don't remember from where or from who,
but I know that when I first heard it, I adopted this
philosophy as my own. If I fail to hit my goals I can feel
very discouraged. If I fail to hit one of my targets, I can
measure how far off from center I am and redesign my
plans or even adjust the target. This is such a significant
difference and can have a profound effect on your
mindset that I encourage all of my clients to set targets
instead of goals.

In addition, your targets need four components:

1. They need to be meaningful to you.
2. They need to be measurable.
3. They need to be achievable.
4. And they need to be exciting to you.

Let's explore these in more detail as we are trying to set ourselves up for success.

## IS YOUR TARGET MEANINGFUL TO YOU?

If you are setting a target that is about making yourself look good to someone else, is it meaningful to you? Or what if you choose a target that someone else convinced you was what was most important but wasn't meaningful to you, would you be motivated to hit that target?

Your target has to mean something to *you*. It has to be important to *you*. A key here, is to go back to your values and personal life themes. Does your target incorporate your values?

For example, if I were just writing this book for the money, either from royalties or from the clients it might attract or I was writing it to get personal accolades, I can tell you, honestly, I would have never been motivated to finish it. There is absolutely nothing wrong with these reasons for writing a book, and they may be meaningful to someone else, but not me.

I was motivated to finish this book, to hit my target of writing and publishing this book, because it aligned with my values of creativity wrapped around wanting to share with and contribute to others.

## IS YOUR TARGET MEASURABLE?

In addition to setting targets that are meaningful to *you*, they need to be measurable. This will help keep you on track and show you how close you are to the bull's-eye. Continuing with my book writing example, I had a target of fourteen chapters, and two thousand words per chapter. I also had a due date for completing the first draft. As I moved through my writing, my targets acted as guides, and the due date helped me focus and stay on track. When I was finished, I was able to measure how close I came to my targets and make adjustments for the next draft. I didn't feel bad if one chapter was one thousand words; it just told me there wasn't enough content in that chapter, and I had to go back and write some more. I felt successful and motivated.

## IS YOUR TARGET ACHIEVABLE AND EXCITING?

Next, your targets need to be achievable and exciting. I'm going to look at these two together, because a lot of people get too excited over *big* targets that aren't necessarily achievable. For example, it doesn't do any good to set an income target of $150,000 for your first year in your event planning business if you never earned more than 10 percent of that in the past six to twelve months. You could hit that target, but is it realistic? You want a target big enough to see, but not so big it obscures everything else from your view. We are aiming for success. We can aim for bigger and bigger targets, but we need to get some wins, feel some successes first.

Several years ago, I was attempting to start a new business with a consulting partner. I'd convinced myself that I needed a partner, someone more outgoing than I was to help get customers.

I'd met a woman through a friend who seemed like a good fit. She was super outgoing, loved to network, and just had this very energetic vibe about her.

She was moving away from teaching and the education sector and wanted to go after clients in the business sector, specifically new start-ups. She'd heard these clients had money to burn, and she wanted a piece of the action. This was the post dot-com boom in the mid-2000s, so there wasn't as much money out there as she imagined.

We set a target of five new clients by the end of the year and a target of $500,000 total – that is, a $100,000 contract with each new client.

Something about this just didn't sit right with me. First, neither of us had ever worked directly with start-ups. Her experience as a consultant was within school systems and my experience was with small distribution companies that were growing but were beyond the initial start-up phase.

The biggest contract she'd ever landed was $30,000 and mine was $10,000.

Five hundred thousand seemed to me a really big stretch. And it didn't align with my values. Money has never been at the top of my list. Yes, I wanted to make a good living, but money isn't the driving force that motivates me. Helping others, supporting their growth, learning, and teaching are what motivates me.

Nothing about these targets felt right. We set a deadline: twelve months. We set monthly targets of how many people we had to talk to and what we thought the conversion rate would be. The targets were clear and measurable. But in my eyes, they were not achievable or exciting.

We clashed over these targets. She was so focused on the dollars and nothing would persuade her otherwise. I tried, but nothing resonated with me; no matter what I said, I could not change her mind. We eventually went our separate ways.

I still enjoyed consulting work, so I set my own targets. As I was consulting as a side business, I set a target of one new contract for $10,000 over the next six months within the distribution industry. My ideal customer was a small company, $500-$1M in revenue, that was experiencing growth and needed to be able to add additional distribution routes and customers without adding new equipment or people and with minimal increase in mileage. At the time, these were the customers that were exciting for me to work with. I loved learning about their business models, I was excited to share my experience, and I could make a difference in their business by helping them expand and stay profitable. It was a win-win.

My targets, unlike those with my business partner,

were meaningful, measurable, achievable, and exciting. Additionally, they aligned with my values and were a good fit for my goals and mission at the time, which was to have a profitable side business, that allowed me to continue to grow and learn while making a difference in the warehousing and distribution industry, an industry I had prior experience in and enjoyed working in.

My target was big enough, but not too big. I could have made it a little bigger, but I knew how much time and energy I had to invest; if I made the target too big, I would have been pushing myself beyond what I could handle and would burn out.

## DOES YOUR TARGET HAVE ALL FOUR COMPONENTS?

When Patrice, whom you met in the previous chapter, set her big target of eventually owning her own event hall, we needed to check in to see if it met all four components: meaningful, measurable, achievable, and exciting.

This was a big target and not one that was going to happen overnight. We knew it wasn't too big, because one of her mentors also owned her own event place, so Patrice felt she could eventually do the same thing.

Was it meaningful to Patrice? Having her own space meant that she would have more control over the timing of her events, the décor, the lighting, the fixtures, the furniture – everything that went into creating an environment that fit the occasion. It was important to her to deliver a memorable experience for her clients, and she knew that having her own space would give her the creative freedom to do this.

She set a target deadline of five years so it was measurable. She could buy it sooner, or maybe a little later, but she had a target to aim for and one to keep her focused.

Next, was it achievable? Patrice knew how much she was generating in revenue now, so she set a budget to save for the down payment. Knowing how much she could generate when she had her own space, she put together a future budget and included it in her business plan to take to the bank for financing when she was ready.

Now she checked off meaningful, measurable, and achievable. Next, was it exciting? Without a doubt. Patrice held the vision of her own space every time she organized a party. She looked at commercial real estate ads. She told friends and family about her target. She told her mentor and she told her clients that in a few years, she'd have the perfect place for their future events. Patrice was not only excited by her target, one that aligned with her dreams and the life she was creating for herself, but she got everyone she talked to excited about her target, too.

## NOT ALL DREAMS AND THEIR TARGETS ARE RELATED TO BUSINESS

Audrey's dream was to travel and to live her life as a nomad. She didn't want to be tied down to one location. There were hundreds of ways she could do this, and we spent several sessions brainstorming. She decided that since adventure was one of her primary values she did not want to work remotely or to work while she traveled.

She did some research and planned a six-month trip around the world. She knew how much money she needed and added some extra as a cushion.

Her first target was traveling for six months. It was meaningful to her because it was a lifelong dream. It was measurable, as she knew how long she wanted to be gone. It was achievable because she had a plan, and she followed blogs of other people who had done what she wanted to do; it was super exciting.

Her second target was savings related. She knew how much money she needed to make her dream come true so she set about earning it, working several jobs at one time. She rented a room from a friend to cut down on her expenses. Her whole focus was saving. It was all meaningful to her because it was a means to an end. She was focused on her savings goal. She knew what she needed and measured how close she was to her savings goal on a weekly basis. Again, she knew it was achievable because she had a plan and others had done it before her. She wasn't too excited about the jobs she was doing, but she was excited by watching her savings grow and getting closer to her target.

It took Audrey eight months, not six to save enough money to travel and her trip only lasted five months instead of six, but her dream had come true and even though she didn't hit the bull's-eye of her target she came close enough to. Now, with some experience under her belt, and feeling successful, Audrey has new, bigger travel and savings targets, all of which fit into the bigger picture of creating the life she wants to live now, instead of in the future, before it's too late.

Now it's your turn. You know what you want, your dreams, the life you want to create. You've taken control of your time. You have the details of what your best life looks like. Now it's time to set some targets.

## JOURNAL QUESTIONS AND EXERCISES

• List three targets directly related to creating the life you want to create. They can be related to money, location, customers, number of followers, word count, and so on.

• Next, under each target write:

> ○ Why is the target meaningful to you?
> ○ How will you measure it?
> ○ What makes you believe it is achievable?
> ○ Why is it exciting?

• Is your target big enough but not too big? In other words, did you pick something too easy or too difficult?

• Do your targets align with your higher purpose, values, and/or mission?

## TIPS AND SUGGESTIONS

• List your targets next to your values and personal life themes to make sure they support one another.

• Check in with yourself periodically to make sure your targets are still meaningful and exciting.

• Keep your targets visible and look at them every day – on your bulletin board, on your computer desktop, anywhere you can read them every day.

• Carry your targets in your purse, wallet, or on your phone and read them whenever you have a few minutes instead of mindlessly scrolling social media.

# KEY #4 – BREAK IT DOWN

*"A dream without a plan is just a wish."*

— SUZY TORONTO

Are you sometimes overwhelmed by a new project or goal? You can see the big picture, but you have no idea where to start.

The key to achieving any dream, reaching a target, or completing any project is to break it down into the smallest possible step, the smallest imaginable piece.

Sounds easier said than done? Maybe not. You probably already do this in some areas of your life and don't even realize it.

Think about it: Are you a mom or a dad? What do you do on a normal school or workday? Lie in bed feeling overwhelmed by all the tasks in front of you – getting up; fixing breakfast; packing lunches; making sure everyone has their homework, laptops, and phones; getting the kids dressed and out the door to meet the school bus on time; letting the dog out, putting the dishes in the dishwasher. The morning to-do could go on and on.

But in some form or other, you do it every day. You start with the smallest task – say making sure the kids are up and moving about, and then you move on from there.

What you do is almost second nature now. However, think back to the first day of school or the first day you returned to work after starting your family. Were you overwhelmed, anxious, running late, feeling unorganized and wondering how you would do it all?

What is the difference between now and then?

Well, first, you recognized you had to figure it out; you didn't have a choice. Then, you tackled the most immediate task, the one right in front of you and then you moved onto the next one. Next, by trial and error, you tried different routines until you found one that worked. And finally, you fell into a practiced routine that you now take for granted.

That's what this chapter is about. We are going to break your big targets down into small steps to move you forward.

Personally, I've used the "breaking it down, taking baby steps" process for years, over and over again when tackling new projects at work. I would simultaneously be working on next year's fiscal budget while developing an operational and financial model to validate a new distribution center and also testing and developing new analysis and tracking programs as well as be writing and planning my next event at home in the evenings.

I applied the same "break it down, make it happen" process in my personal life to plan a vacation, start a remodeling or redecorating project, or just to organize my massive library. It was particularly helpful when we decided to move three thousand miles across the country.

When people would ask me how I did it all, I began to share my "secret." People loved the idea so much because it was effective. It is so second nature to me now that when I wanted to officially teach it, I had to apply the same steps.

There are two methods I use to start breaking down targets into action steps. Both are similar and use a technique I call "brainstorm free-flow writing."

## OUTLINES AND LISTS

This is just what it sounds like – an outline or a list. Mine aren't all that neat and don't really resemble any outline you may have seen in school, but it helps me get everything out of my head and onto paper.

This process can take a few days. You begin by writing your target at the top of a sheet of paper. Next try to list as many subcategories as you can think of.

Then under each subcategory list more ideas, steps, questions, tasks, and so on.

For me this can be spread across several different pages and notebooks, index cards, sticky notes, and similar.

Once you start this process, even when you are not sitting down writing, it will never leave your subconscious. New ideas, to-dos, tasks, questions, and such can float to the surface anytime – while driving, cleaning, cooking, eating lunch, sitting in a meeting, talking to a friends, or watching TV. It is very important to have pens and paper easily accessible at all times.

The next step is to set aside an hour or so to sit down with all of your notes, sort them, and try to organize them. You can then move to your laptop and type all the information up if you haven't already started.

This serves two purposes: first, as you are typing your notes, you will get more ideas, and second, as you continue to refine what you need to do, you will also begin to actually build the project and take some steps without even realizing it. Typing your notes also serves a third purpose: all of your notes are now in one place, and you can cut and paste easily to reorganize them.

This is the exact process Janet and I used when we rented the condo at the shore to help her begin her new business.

First, we did a brain dump of everything she wanted to do, to teach, who she wanted to teach, steps she might have to take. We didn't try to organize anything. We didn't question, judge, minimize, reject, or criticize anything. We used notebooks, giant sticky notes on the walls, and index cards.

We brainstormed more ideas and more steps and added to everything we already had.

Next, we needed to choose one target to break down into action steps.

Janet found this a little overwhelming. She felt like everything had to be done right now, and she didn't know where to begin.

We looked at her targets related to her dream of teaching workshops and seminars to help women transition into new careers and to empower them to take control of their future.

• Host a three-day retreat (like what we were doing) at a B&B at the shore for up to eight women.

• Generate at least $50,000 in the next twelve months from the business.

• Be invited to speak at least once a month at local Kiwanis clubs, network groups, Chamber of Commerce, and similar venues.

• Launch a new website.

• Begin posting on Facebook daily.

• Travel to North Carolina at least twice a month to spend time with her family.

Janet wanted to accomplish a lot.

First we tabled traveling to North Carolina because although it was important to her, it wasn't related to starting her business. This made her sad, and I tried to discuss it with her; however, at the time, she insisted on working on her business. For the moment, I let it go. This was her weekend, and she was the client. Still, I tucked this information away to circle back to later.

Next, we looked at what was needed for her to be successful in her new business.

Number one was that she needed clients: women to attend her workshops and seminars.

No one knew who she was, what she had to share, or why they should pay to work with her.

She didn't know the women she wanted to work with. Where were they and how could she reach them?

We decided together that the first step was to focus on getting invitations to speak. Janet thought she had to have a website first. I agreed she needed a website but not that it was what she needed first. When she pushed back, I asked her how her website would reach the women she wanted to work with. She gave a long answer that included using Facebook and posting blogs that were search engine optimized. All good steps but not the first one.

First we had to get her in front of other women so they could get to know her in person. Her workshops and seminars were going to be in person, so she needed to start meeting women in her region and could grow an audience from there.

She agreed, and we decided to focus on being invited to speak at least once a month at local Kiwanis clubs, network groups, and Chamber of Commerce meetings.

This started a new round of brainstorming, and we came up with a list of small action steps she could start right away.

• Make a list of every group she could potentially speak in front of.

• Make a list of topics to talk about and choose one or two as her foundation.

• Email, call, or write a letter to at least one group or person every day.

• Outline and write her presentation.

• Join her local Toastmasters to practice her presentation.

• Invite a group of supportive friends to her home and practice her presentation.

• Ask her friends for names or referrals for groups she could speak in front of.

These first small steps got Janet moving forward, and before the weekend was over, we had her list of topics, had chosen the two she'd use as a foundation, and she had emailed her friends to schedule a lunch date at her home before the end of the month. She knew exactly what she needed to do (draft her first presentation), she knew her topic, and she had a time frame in which to complete it (before her lunch date at the end of the month).

We continued over the weekend to refine and break down each target, making sure each one was meaningful, measurable, achievable, and exciting. Each target had five to ten steps to take. If there were more steps than that, the target was too big, and we broke the target down into two or more targets.

Janet felt great. She'd moved from feeling overwhelmed and not sure where to start to having targets aligned with her dream and the action steps to go with them. She felt focused, confident, and in control.

## MIND MAPS

The second tool I use to begin breaking things down into small action steps is very similar to the outlines and lists: mind maps. The difference is that mind maps are more visual and contained, not spread out over multiple notebooks, index cards, and sticky notes.

First, start with a really *big* piece of paper, poster size if possible. Have lots of colored sharpies, pencils, and pens handy to make it fun. Get everything in your head and out onto the paper. Every idea, project, and task you can think of. This includes all personal-, work-, and business-related stuff. It all comes out here. Use arrows and shapes to connect ideas.

Do you like words, pictures, shapes? Do whatever you need to here to get everything out of your head and onto the paper in a way that is meaningful and inspiring to *you*. Mind maps are most often used by people who are visual and respond better to color and images.

Next, start breaking down things. Personal. Business. Work. Use highlighters to differentiate each category.

What's most important in this moment related to your dream, the life you want to create? Is it in the personal, business, or work area?

For most people I work with, it is in their business, or the business they want to start, so we will pull out one idea and start a new mind map, maybe on a smaller piece of paper. These are what I call focused mind maps.

And just as we did with the outlines and lists, we'll start adding steps, numbering them, and adding timelines and dates. Use a highlighter for the target and circle and number the related steps. If a target has to be broken down into more than five to ten steps to be achievable, break down the target into two or more targets and start a new mind map.

Next, we need to start taking all of this information and create a list with timelines that you can add to your calendar and carry with you at all times. This is where the two methods – outlines and lists and mind maps – begin to merge.

What we are doing basically here is taking all the

work you've done so far and breaking it all down so you can begin moving toward the life you want and bring your dreams to life.

You have your big dream and the big targets that support that dream. Then the big targets are broken down into smaller targets that are meaningful, measurable, achievable, and exciting. Then each small target is broken down into five to ten tasks, or action steps, each with an assigned timeline and deadline. You will then move back up to the small target and assign a deadline and then move up to the big target and assign a deadline. Each target and associated action step has a time period in which to act and complete the task.

I know this too can feel a little overwhelming. That's why sometimes it's good to do it with a friend or coach. Once you get going, the process is fun, and once you start taking action, crossing things off your list and experiencing things happening, it will be even more fun.

## DAILY TO-DO LIST

The final step is to create your daily to-do list. The key is that the to-do list never exceeds one page. That means there is a lot of scratching out, reorganizing, and prioritizing along the way.

I've used this process over and over again through the years, and it's never failed to keep me focused, moving forward and finding success. I know each day what I'm going to do and why.

At the end of every day I review what I've done and what I didn't complete. Everything not accomplished on the first list goes to the top of a new list for the next day. I have a master list of steps that I need to take to move me forward to meet my target by the due date. I use this list to create my next day's plan.

One additional thing I'll share with you about my to-do lists is that I like to use a single notepad or notebook. I start a new to-do list by turning the page. By saving my old lists, I can see how much I've accomplished over days, weeks, and months.

By managing my to-do lists in a single place it ends up becoming a nice reminder of how much I've accomplished, especially when I have days when I hit a lot of road bumps.

And, I promise you, you will hit a few road bumps along the way, and we will cover those in the next chapter.

Each item on your to-do list is a small action step that moves you toward your target and your dream. You are building the life you want one moment, one step, at a time.

By keeping all of your action steps and to-do lists together in a single notebook, you can see just how close you are to your target and how much further you have to go.

This step is so critical to your success, to creating the life you want; please don't skip it thinking you know what you need to do and it's all in your head. Get it out onto paper. Add your timelines. Measure your progress. Celebrate your wins. Start over when you need to. But keep taking one step at a time, and I have no doubt you will be successful at reclaiming and living your dreams.

## JOURNAL QUESTIONS AND EXERCISES

• Are your targets directly related to your dream? If not, why? Is your dream what you really want? Explore your thoughts and feelings in your journal and with your coach.

• Are your targets meaningful, measurable, achievable, and exciting?

• How are your small steps moving you forward?

• Explore how this step, of breaking down your targets into action steps with timelines makes you feel. Explore these thoughts and feelings with your therapist, a good friend, or your coach.

## TIPS AND SUGGESTIONS

• Make this exercise fun. Use big paper, colored pens, markers, and pencils.

• Use words and images to help bring your ideas and

targets to life. You can draw them or cut them from magazines.

• Keep all your to-do lists in one notebook. Review it to see how far you've come.

• If you feel overwhelmed by this step, work with a good friend or your coach to help you.

## KEY #5 – PLAN FOR MISSTEPS

*"It is constant effort and hard work – and inexplicably life-affirming – to honor who you are, what you believe, and why you are here."*

— ELLE LUNA

Obstacles and road blocks: "I've fallen and I can't get up."

You're going to hit bumps, take missteps, stumble, and fall down.

Taking small steps, facing obstacles and roadblocks, starting again, and taking small steps has shown me that living your life purpose instead of merely existing means that you will no longer be on cruise control, drifting down a calm river.

Living means experiencing it all; it means traveling the white water and "shooting the rapids." Emotional highs and lows are part of the journey, part of living.

Notice I didn't say good or bad. There are cycles to everything – emotions, energy, the wind. The highs and lows are neither good nor bad; they are just part of the cycle.

As you begin taking small steps, you'll run into obstacles and roadblocks.

You'll hit a bump, stumble, and fall.

You'll take a misstep, make a mistake.

It's bound to happen. It happens to us all.

How you handle them will determine how fast you get moving again.

The most important key in the beginning is to just start moving.

Now let's imagine you're cruising right along, taking small steps every day.

You're thinking, "Hey, this isn't as hard as I thought it'd be."

You're feeling elated, euphoric really. You've acted despite your fear and anxiety, and you're wondering what took you so long to get moving in the first place.

This is about the time you hit your first wall or trip and fall down. You're shaken, confused, not sure what is happening. It suddenly feels like everyone and everything is conspiring against you, trying to stop you.

Take a deep breath and relax. Obstacles and road blocks are a natural part of the journey. As a matter of fact, taking three steps forward and two steps back is a pretty average dance, especially in the early stages.

You have to be prepared for these setbacks and not let them stop you.

## STRATEGIES FOR GETTING BACK ON TRACK AFTER A MISSTEP

There are several strategies that can help you get back on track and moving again after a misstep.

• Reach out. We've talked about support in a previous chapter. This is the time to use it. Sometimes you need to talk to someone who understands. Having a circle of support, people who understand what you are doing and why, is essential. Now is the time to tap this support, reach out and talk to someone. Sometimes that's all it takes to get on your feet again and start taking small steps again. You just need someone to hear you, see you, and witness what is happening.

• Ask for help. Sometimes, you'll need to ask for help. Again, turn to your circle of support. Put what you need out there and be specific. Do you need help with technology, a resource, spreading the word? Ask for help.

• Inspiration. Go to the well of inspiration often. You need reminders, and you need to stay inspired to keep moving forward.

• Know why. Understanding your own motivation and the reasons behind it is very important. It's also important to write it down and carry it with you to refer to as often as necessary to give you the continuing courage you'll need to keep taking small steps, even if it feels like you are moving backward sometimes.

• Take a break. Sometimes when you are hitting road-block after roadblock and are having trouble figuring out how to get around them or move through them, it's best to just take a break, walk away for a bit, and have a little fun. Reread Chapter 4, Self-Care: Slow Down to Speed Up. You'll be surprised when the answers to your problems just seem to pop into your head or you have a sudden insight or clarity.

• Get quiet. Sometimes you just have to sit with the obstacle and see what it is trying to tell you. Maybe you took a misstep and need to change directions. Maybe you need to slow down. To hear the message the obstacle is trying to send you, you may just need to get quiet, sit silently, and see what comes up.

## OBSTACLES AND ROADBLOCKS: MORE WAYS YOU CAN STUMBLE

It's not just missteps that can have you falling down; sometimes obstacles and roadblocks can trip you up.

Some of the obstacles and roadblocks I've encountered are a lack of knowledge or skill set, technical issues and snafus, losses and failures, and timing issues. Other obstacles I've faced revolve around my own self-doubt and the emotional highs and lows associated with living instead of merely existing.

Some examples of the technical obstacles I've faced over the years include my web server crashing, my laptop crashing, and my website being hacked several times. Each and every time, I had to start over.

In the personal realm I've lost some key supporters and friends along the way. People who I thought were on my side, cheering me along, suddenly just disappeared. I'm not even sure why in some cases. It hurt, but I had to let it go and move on.

My own self-doubt has been a huge battle and obstacle. I've felt like quitting and running away many times and on a few occasions came very close to chucking it all. It's hard when you suddenly start acknowledging your dreams, your life purpose, who you are, and who you want to be and committing to make a difference in the world. Everything in your psyche can fight back, trying to keep things the same. Growing is hard. Growing pains are real.

And, sometimes, missteps, especially in the beginning, are just due to inexperience.

## MISSTEPS ARE LEARNING OPPORTUNITIES

One of the missteps I took once, early on (beyond choosing a business partner who didn't share my values), was working without a contract. Who does that? Well, I did because I wanted to prove to my first potential new customer that I could do what I was saying I could do. Big misstep.

The company was about six hours away in Maryland, and the owner needed new delivery routes as he'd picked up several new customers in the past few months. I loved figuring things out, so I gathered up all his delivery addresses, fleet information, and delivery time windows and went to work. Then, instead of telling him what the results could be before actually turning the new delivery models over to him, I just sent him the new models. Big misstep. Obviously, he now had what he wanted. We hadn't signed a contract, so although I did the work, I didn't get paid.

This felt like a big misstep, and I started beating myself up. Then I stopped, stepped back, and reached out for support from a friend in a similar business. He made me realize that although I'd lost some time and didn't get paid, the experience hadn't really cost me anything, and it was a great learning experience. Doing the work gave me confidence, and I was able to bounce back.

Jocelyn faced a similar misstep when she organized her first painting retreat for women with breast cancer. She decided she wanted to host her first retreat in the fall. The weather at the beach would still be warm but not overly hot, and most of the families with children would be gone as the kids would be back in school. She picked a date, did her research, and found a nice B&B that could support up to twelve women. So far so good.

Jocelyn was so intent on following through on delivering the best experience she could to the women who came to her retreat, she'd not focused enough on the backend and how much running the retreat would cost her. The retreat itself was a success. She loved leading the women through different painting exercises and the feedback they gave her told her she was on the right track. She was following her dreams and creating the life she wanted, but she miscalculated and ended up losing money. This was not a part of the dream.

Losing money felt like a big blow. Not only did it mean she had to keep her job longer than expected to pay off the debt she'd incurred on her credit cards, she began to question if this really was something she was meant to do.

We talked about it and revisited her dreams and targets. She found support in the feedback from her retreat attendees and circle of friends. She slowed down and looked at how she had miscalculated. The catered meals were more expensive than she budgeted for, and at the last minute she'd added a yoga instructor and energy healer to give the women more support but hadn't included these costs in her budget. Everything she'd done was because she was focused on her clients, which is a god thing, but she forgot to include herself, which meant making a profit, in her considerations.

She also had to ask herself why she'd "forgotten" to include these extra expenses. Working together, we uncovered some money biases Jocelyn held. Together we explored her false beliefs around charging for helping people. She had to let go of the belief that she shouldn't be making money from someone's tragedy and start looking at her retreats as beneficial opportunities to support another person's health and well-being. They were a service that was valuable.

It took Jocelyn a few months to recover from her misstep, but she learned from it. Her next retreat, although smaller, was profitable, and she continued to move forward.


## MISSTEPS ARE INEVITABLE

Missteps are going to happen. You are going to trip and fall down. I shared how I did all the work for a consulting client before getting a contract signed and never got paid for the work I did and how Jocelyn undercharged for her services.

Both of us felt like failures. We both beat ourselves up. But that doesn't help. It doesn't move you forward. Reframing the situation from a failure to a misstep is helpful. You can't fall into the trap of criticizing yourself or judging yourself. Imagine seeing your child take their first step and fall flat on its behind. Would you tell them, "Oh, well, you're not good at it, best to just give up." No! Then why criticize yourself? Look at the situation and see what you can learn from it.

When you take a misstep, break it down. Ask yourself what happened. Can it be prevented in the future? What can you do in the future to avoid this particular misstep? Do you need additional resources or support?

My biggest advice here that has worked for me is to not do it alone. You have to have support. No one succeeds on their own despite the American myth of individualism and the "self-made man." It is a myth and a lie and an entire book could be written about the damage this hoax has caused. Trust me on this. When it's hard, ask for support. Sometimes you will be too close to see what needs to be done. Sometimes you will need a break, to rest. Give yourself some space. Step back. Ask for support. It's a sign of maturity and strength, not a sign of weakness. We all are going to fall down sometimes; the trick is to get up and keeping creating the life you want and moving toward your dreams.

## JOURNAL QUESTIONS AND EXERCISES

• When you've fallen down in the past and taken a misstep, how did you handle it? What did you say to yourself? How did you move forward?

• If you were to do it over, what would you say to yourself? What created the opportunity for the misstep to occur? Is this something that could happen again and if so, using what you've learned, what can you do to prevent it?

• Make a list of missteps you've taken in the past and what you learned from them

• Now, imagine a situation where you've fallen, taken a misstep on your path to reclaiming your dream; how

will you handle this differently now? Make a list of
steps you will take to get yourself back on track.


TIPS AND SUGGESTIONS

• Read a biography or autobiography of someone you
admire. How did they manage their missteps? How can
you use their example to inspire yourself to get
back up?

# 13

## KEY #6 – DREAM BIGGER

*"A creative life is an amplified life. It's a bigger life, a happier life, an expanded life, and a hell of a lot more interesting life."*

— ELIZABETH GILBERT

What do you do when you achieve all the targets you've set out to achieve? What happens when you experience the success you've dreamed of? What's next when you are earning a living, making a difference, and doing what you love?

When I've found myself in this position, others have told me to rest, enjoy the moment, and relax. This lasted about two minutes before I became restless and out of sorts.

I can appreciate my successes and celebrate reaching

milestones. I also know how to take a break and be in the moment. I know the importance of slowing down, resting, relaxing, and having the time to rejuvenate my body, mind, and spirit.

But they are all aspects of the journey. Not the end point.

I'm a creator. I'm a dreamer. I'm a doer. And I suspect many of you are, too.

## DREAM BIGGER

So, what do you do?

This is when life can get even better.

You've heard the phrase rinse and repeat? Well, that is where you are now. You get to choose how long you stay where you are, and where you want to go next.

I've had more jobs and side hustle than a dozen people combined. I've had four distinct and different careers. I learned from all of them. I took what I loved about each and expanded it. I've been doing this for decades.

For example, when I worked in retail in my early twenties, I'd master the job, get promoted, master that job, get promoted, resign, and go through the same process somewhere else. I hated being bored, and I loved to learn. But I was trading one low-paying job for another. I then took a factory job. Not a lifelong dream, but it paid really well. My target was to return to school.

I'd only been with the company for a few months when a job notice was posted on the board. This was a union shop, so all jobs had to be posted. You applied for the position, and the person with the most seniority was given the job. The position posted paid almost twice what I made, was one of the highest-paying positions on the production floor, and came with mandatory overtime. In other words, two hours a day at time and half at twice the rate I was currently making. All I saw were dollar signs. At first, I wasn't going to apply as I was really the next-to-lowest man on the totem pole with no seniority. But most of the people I worked with had been with the company for years and did not want to work as hard as this position required. I took a chance and applied. No one else did, so I got the job.

It was intense. The factory made butter and margarine, cold milk, cream, salt, and hot oil. My job was to maintain the giant cold tanks of milk, cream, and salt. It meant monitoring the ammonia levels to maintain the tank temperature and the mix ratios and adjusting everything as needed. For weeks I followed around the older guy who was training taking notes. I loved to learn, and this was something completely new.

After a few weeks, the job was mine. I loved not being confined to the production line. I loved the autonomy and independence of the position, and I actually liked the responsibility. And I loved the money.

A few things came out of this job, which by the way, and pretty obviously, wasn't my life work. However, I did confirm again to myself that I was good at learning and adapting to new things. I realized that autonomy and independence were a must-have in future employment opportunities, and I realized that not everyone is willing to take on responsibility so that gave me an advantage.

During the time I held this position, I saved most of my paychecks. My target was to save enough money to finish my degree and not have to work. After six months I had the money, I had new insights about myself, and I was ready to go back to school and finish my nutrition degree. At the time, I believed that my interests in food and nutrition were going to be my life work. It didn't quite turn out that way, but again it was a step on the journey and to an ever-expanding vision of what was possible.

## RINSE AND REPEAT

A few years ago, I reconnected with Rita, from Chapter 1. She was living her dream life, her very best life, but something wasn't quite right. Her event planning company was fully booked a year out with fundraisers for local and even a few national charities. She and her husband had purchased the property she had fallen in love with and most of her events were held in the large barn on the property. She was living her dream. She was living a life of purpose and meaning. Her business was making money and making a difference at the same time. She'd created the life she wanted, yet at the same time, she felt unsettled and agitated at times and didn't know why.

This is when I shared with Rita the concept of rinse and repeat, expanding her dream. You've heard the phrase "it's the journey, not the destination that counts"? That's where Rita was and where I'd found myself numerous times over the years.

After I completed my degree in nutrition and began what I considered my second career, the first being in retail, I took a job at a local hospital. My job was to manage the kitchen staff, review new patients' charts, make dietary recommendations based on their condition, and do patient education. I hated it. I thought I'd love helping people realize the power of food and nutrition. This wasn't the case. The rules were so strict, and the people were so sick that I couldn't make an impact.

I also realized I was empathic and absorbed all the suffering I came into contact with. After about two and a half years, I changed hospitals, but it wasn't much better. In this second position, I took on some new responsibilities, which included developing and teaching the monthly required continuing education for the kitchen staff. I fell in love with the process of creating and developing a curriculum and teaching. No one else wanted to do it, so I never had to share this responsibility. I loved it so much I'd often work on the lessons in my free time and wasn't paid for it.

In addition to realizing that I loved to create and teach, I discovered I had a real talent for operational efficiency. I'd watch the food line and move people around so we could assemble the meal trays more quickly.

In the office, it was required that every new patient be seen and charted within twenty-four hours. It was also a target, one we rarely met, to get the menu selections from all patients for all meals. When you are in the hospital, you have so little control over what is happening to you and when that selecting your own meals was very empowering.

In my free time I created a new schedule to maximize patient charting time and menu selection. I presented it to the chief dietician, and she agreed. There was push back from the staff, as the new schedule eliminated a lot of the downtime and transferred some of the nonessential duties to the kitchen staff. Within weeks of implementing my plans, we had increased new patient charting within twenty-four hours to 99 percent, from 65 percent, and menu selection from 60 to 70 percent to 100 percent on many days with an average of 98 to 99 percent. This was phenomenal. And we did it without adding people or hours to the schedule.

I loved this aspect of my job, but I hated working in the hospital. Like I said, the pain and suffering I observed was taking its toll, and I had to leave. The efficiency projects and teaching were just distractions to delay the inevitable. I had to resign. It was time to rinse and repeat, to take all the good, set new targets, dream a new dream, and start over.

And that's what I did. I loved to teach, and I was good at observing and making changes to improve productivity and efficiency. I enjoyed working in an office environment. This was a surprise to me. I'd rebelled and resisted "women's" work since high school, refusing to take business or typing classes and instead took drafting for four years (the only girl in my class). So, up until I worked at the hospital, I'd taken jobs in warehouse, factories, and retail, mostly manual labor. After working at the hospital, I realized how much I loved to use my brain, my intellect, and my creativity.

This new awareness once again led me to a new and expanded vision. Not only did I apply for and get an office position, which led to many more promotions and two new careers, but it gave me a new vision for my life outside of work, and the foundation for the side hustles I continually started, played with, and learned from. My expanded vision included writing, teaching, and sharing what I learned. It's the foundation of every-thing I do today and the driving force behind every new dream, new vision, and the life I'm creating for myself.

That's what I wanted for Rita. We started working together again. She needed a new, expanded vision of what was possible, what was next. She didn't want to stop what she was doing; she really did love the plan-ning fundraising events, but she needed more. She needed another outlet for her creativity. Plus, she'd learned in the previous years as she was building her business that she loved to mentor others. She also real-ized she was an excellent manager. She was excellent at seeing not only the big picture but also all the details that went with it, and she discovered she could not only train and delegate the details she enjoyed it.

We decided to brainstorm around this new awareness – training and delegating and mentoring others. Rita and I played with a lot of ideas, one of which was to sell her business and start something new, but after sitting with it, Rita decided against it. She still thrived on planning fundraising events, she just needed more. She needed an expanded vision.

Rita eventually decided to promote, train, and mentor two of the women who'd worked with her almost from the beginning and who loved what they did as much as she did. Over the next twelve months, Rita worked with them, giving them more and more responsibility until one day they were managing the day-to-day running of the company.

"Now what?" Rita asked me.

"Rinse and repeat." I answered. "Rinse and repeat," Rita laughed.

Rita knew now how to expand her dream, and she began to work with other event planners and fundraising managers from around the country, sharing her knowledge and mentoring others who shared her vision.

Just like Rita, and many of my other clients, I've hit that wall and asked the question, "Now what?"

In each of my careers and each side hustle, I was living out my life purpose and, at the same time, giving space for it to expand again and again. I'm a master at the rinse, repeat, and expand process.

Today, I have a sense of purpose and meaning in my life and a feeling of immense joy and gratitude as I'm able to incorporate all the things I love, my past experiences and my interests in ways that empower, educate, inspire, and entertain others. I've been able to do this in my current career and side hustle.

My expanded vision included leaving my career behind and embracing my business as a foundation to serve others while continuing to grow and learn. My expanded vision includes not just me and a business but an organization that embodies my life mission of alleviate the suffering that comes from living a life devoid of purpose and meaning and by empowering others to make a living, while making a difference doing what they love.

My vision is still expanding, as is the vision of many of my clients.

Jocelyn, whom you met in Chapter 7, is considering partnering with organizations, health care providers, and hospitals to offer her painting experiences to more groups of people, not just breast cancer patients and survivors.

Patrice, from Chapter 9, is working with other women business owners to offer to teach the younger people in their communities how to dream big, build their own businesses, and buy property, helping create generational wealth.

And Audrey, whom you learned about in Chapter 10, is not only dreaming about traveling but is considering the possibilities of what it would be like to live outside of the country permanently.

Never stop dreaming. Let your dreams continue to grow and expand.


## JOURNAL QUESTIONS AND EXERCISES

• Make a list of all the jobs, degrees, careers, and businesses you've had and list under them what you loved about each and what you disliked.

• What specific talents, interests, or knowledge stand out?

• What other insights or awareness can you see now looking back?

• How can you take what you know, apply it to your dream, and expand it?

• What does your expanded vision look like, feel like? Lean into the possibilities and play with them.


## TIPS AND SUGGESTIONS

• Who do you know who has lived multiple life purposes, pursued multiple careers, or had success in different fields?

• If they are someone you know, or someone you'd like to know, could you invite them out to coffee or lunch and ask them to tell you about themselves?

• Can you follow them on social media, subscribe to their newsletter or YouTube channel, or read their book?

# 14

## OBSTACLES, THE SLIPPERY SLOPE OF GOING BACK TO "NORMAL"

*"No matter what you tell the world or tell yourself, your actions reveal your real values. Your actions show you what you really want."*

— DEREK SIVERS

Y ou've made it this far. Congratulations! You've learned the tools to take back control of your life:

• You explored how important self-care is and how slowing down allows you to speed up and take back control of your life.

• You looked at your top values and personal life themes and began using them as a guiding light to make choices and decisions to stay on track.

• Although it was sometimes uncomfortable, you began to delegate tasks to others and share the load giving you more control over your time.

• And finally, you began to identify and ask for the support you needed and recognized how important this was to regaining control of your time and your life.

You've learned the steps to manifest your dreams and life purpose:

1. Visualize the Details: Fleshing Out the Dream
2. Determine the Right Time
3. Set Your Targets
4. Break It Down
5. Plan for Missteps
6. Dream Bigger

Now, reality may be setting in. This is hard work. There are no easy-peasy answers. It takes time, awareness, accountability, action, and daily commitment.

To live is a verb; to live your life purpose and your dreams, you need to take action. You can't just sit back and visualize yourself to success. Visualization, as we talked about, needs to be combined with movement, action, and doing something.

We talked about the obstacles that will come up and slow you down, trip you up, make you think and feel like you want to quit.

These are all the reasons why the majority of people

only talk about their life purpose and big dreams. They quit before they ever start. They imagine the obstacles will be too big to overcome, or the sacrifice too much. They convince themselves that it, the cost to be paid, isn't worth it. They cannot see themselves taking sustained action day after day, investing in themselves, and being willing to look deeply into who they are, and why they do things. The majority of people want easy, and this ain't easy.

If you've made it this far, you are in the minority. First, most people will start books but don't finish them. Most people will read a book but not do the exercise. I think you are different. I imagine you holding this book in your hands or looking at it on your Kindle reader with a notebook and pen beside you or your laptop open with all your notes, ideas, plans, and steps written out. I also imagine you now sitting back and realizing, "Whoa, this is a lot of work."

This is when you might start telling yourself your current life isn't too bad. You've implemented some of the techniques to take back control of your life, and you now have more time; you feel more in control, and you're not feeling overwhelmed. You're feeling pretty good.

You start to tell yourself that your job isn't that bad; your relationships are "working"; you have more time for yourself; you feel contented.

But is that what you really want? For your life to be OK, to just feel contented? If you answered yes, then read no further. You've gotten what you needed from this book and from me. Congratulations.

But if your yes is tinged with a question mark, or your stomach twists in knots when you say yes, or you have a no, then read on.

This is a precarious time. This is when you are starting to really see the possibilities and how it is going to change your life and the lives of those closest to you. This is when those around you are going to really start pushing back. Most people don't like change, and they certainly don't like change when they have no control over it.

You are changing. Your life is changing. The lives of the people closest to you is changing. There is going to be big resistance to this change internally and exter- nally. This is the moment when it is so easy to slip back into your old normal. It feels comfortable, like your old college sweatshirt. It feels great on a cold day when you don't have to leave the house. It's also stained, has holes in it, and, in all honesty, doesn't really look or fit all that well anymore. Yes, it's comfortable, but do you really want it to be a part of your everyday wardrobe?

I get it. You feel like you are standing alone, blowing in the wind. Most people aren't going to understand what you are trying to do or trying to create and at times you aren't going to understand either.

This point in your journey is so crucial.

This is where you need to come back to your daily practice and remind yourself every day what you are doing and why you are doing it. This is when you need to circle back to your support team and share what you are thinking and feeling. These are the days you just have to get up and put one foot in front of the other and ride the wave. Right now that wave may be pummeling you and you are feeling like just letting go, but if you stay with it, ride the waves of feelings, thoughts and emotions, eventually, I promise, you come out on the other side riding a new wave, one of joy, determination, purpose and meaning. You need to stay with each wave and ride it. Neither is good or bad, they are just different, and they are each part of the journey and what everyone else goes through, even if social media has convinced us that people only experience one or the other.

I remember the first time I decided to step into a new dream. I'd long dreamed of writing, teaching, and having my own business. My journals were full of ideas, plans, and to-do lists.

After my dad died at fifty-five years old, never having fulfilled all of his dreams, I realized I didn't want to die and never having tried to live out my dreams.

It wasn't just that I had a desire to write and teach; I felt it was a calling. I wanted to change my life, and I wanted to help others do the same. I loved everything about business and wanted the freedom of working for myself and the freedom to write about and teach whatever I wanted.

I knew that financially I couldn't just quit my job, as I was responsible not just for myself and my family but also my mom.

I decided I'd start on the side and see what happened. The term *side-hustle* wasn't as popular then as it is now, but that's what I was doing.

So, I made a commitment to begin taking action on my dreams and targets. Lifelong learning and personal growth were two of my highest values, so one of my first action steps was to attend educational workshops and seminars.

I registered for a workshop entitled "Compelling Storytelling: A New Approach to Marketing" in Las Vegas. It was taught by the late Barbara J. Winter, author of *Making a Living without a Job: Winning Ways for Creating Work That You Love*.

This workshop met all of my criteria: it had a writing component, it was an opportunity to meet like-minded people, it was an opportunity to learn about marketing (an important skill if I was going to manage a successful business), and it would immerse me in a learning environment with a great teacher.

I realize now that the decision to attend was the only easy thing about the entire experience.

By the time I arrived at my hotel, an eighty-hour workweek that didn't end until I turned off my phone in the taxi combined with a three-hour time difference had taken its toll. I was exhausted.

I was still on Jersey time when I awoke the next morning. It was 2:30 a.m. Vegas time.

The meeting notice at the front desk said the workshop started 9:00 a.m. Since I had been waiting for over six hours already, I arrived early and ready to begin. I was politely informed they were not ready, and we would start at 9:30.

I had no sense of time. I had no watch. I wasn't adjusting easily to the three-hour time difference. I hadn't yet cut the invisible cord tying me to the office, and the stress of the past week still had me in its grip.

*Once the workshop started, I would be fine*, or so I told myself. How was I to know that Barbara Winter was an entrepreneurial free spirit?

No agenda was provided. There were no preplanned breaks. There were no clocks in the room. And there were only eight attendees and no place to hide. Plus, this was a hands-on, fully interactive workshop. There was nothing in the brochure about that! Within minutes of starting, we were pairing up and engaging in creative activities and sharing our life stories.

My heart was pounding; the lymph nodes behind my ears were swelling, as they often do when I am stressed; and I was awash in a nervous sweat.

By the time we broke for lunch, my head was spinning. I collapsed into a luxurious, comfortable lobby chair and called my husband, "I think I made a mistake." That's all I said. That's all I could think of. I didn't belong here. All of these women were highly accomplished, ran their own businesses, traveled both domestically and abroad, had lived all over the country, and seemed so at ease with a workshop I was finding very intense and disorienting.

I was definitely in the wrong place.

Regardless of how lost I felt, nature still calls, and

since we only had an eight-minute break and I had used up countless minutes already, I headed toward the ladies room.

Another woman, whose role as an attendee or copresenter I could not figure out, spotted me and asked, "How are you doing?" Her seemingly perceptive grasp of my emotional state had me expressing my distress.

After hearing my laments, with a knowing smile and a mischievous tilt to her head, she said: "Welcome to the world of entrepreneurship!" The comment stopped me in my tracks!

This *is* what I was here for! I *wasn't* in the wrong place. I desperately craved the personal freedom that came from living my dreams and building the life I wanted, being a writer and successful entrepreneur.

My insides relaxed slightly, and I vowed to myself not to give up, to relax into the moment and to be present, to go with the flow, and to trust that this is where I was meant to be. I vowed to myself in that moment, I wasn't going to slip back into my old normal. If I wanted to live out my life purpose, to live the life of my dreams I needed to ride the wave of discomfort. Each morning when I woke up, I said little prayer, wrote in my journal and reminded myself why I was there.

What came out of that event were lifelong friendships and my first business, the Dreaming Café. The tagline was "where self-discovery, self-expression, and self-employment come together." For the next three years, I worked on this business as a side hustle. I wrote almost every day, published over five hundred blog posts and one hundred newsletter articles. I taught teleclasess on journaling for self-discovery, art journaling, and creative self-expression. (If you're not sure what a teleclass is, imagine a Zoom call with no video). I spoke and taught classes to local small business organizations and even worked with a handful of small business owners. Several years later, in 2010, I helped Barbara organize and lead an event for entrepreneurs in Austin, Texas, where we had attendees from all over the United States, Canada, and Great Britain.

The whole experience from attending the workshop, to starting my first business, experiencing what it was like to *live* my life's purpose and to leading an event with a rock star entrepreneur like Barbara was truly a dream come true.

After this experience, I never wanted to go back to what others considered my "normal" life. Since then, I've let go of and started several more side hustles, learned to live my life purpose in whatever work I was doing, and now today live an expanded version of my very first business and live a very unnormal life.

This is what I want for you! I want you to take back your dreams, reclaim your time and energy, and begin creating the life you want to live before it's too late.

I know what it's like to begin dreading Monday morning on Sunday night. I know what it's like to slog through your day helping everyone else achieve their dreams at the expense of your own.

And I know you do, too.

It doesn't have to be that way.

I've changed my life. My clients have changed their lives.

I've shared my story and the stories of my clients.

Do you see yourself in those stories?

We knew what we wanted, and we took action.

You can too.

You can take back your dreams.

You can reclaim your time and your energy.

You can live a life of purpose and meaning.

You can create the life you want before it's too late.

I know you can.

I believe in you.

# ACKNOWLEDGMENTS

I've always been anxious about naming people who have played important roles in my life as I'm afraid to miss someone, but I'm going to give it a try. If you're not on the list, it's not because you aren't important to me; it's just that I have limited room to write and a memory like Swiss cheese sometimes.

First, I want to thank Dr. Angela Lauria for founding and leading Difference Press Publishing and The Author Incubator. Angela's authenticity, heart, and intellect inspire me with every interaction. She is passionate, funny, and fierce. She embodies what it means to be a good leader – someone who leads by lifting others up and giving them space to shine while supporting a shared vision. I would not have been able to finish this book without her encouragement, leadership, and vision.

And her team shines just as bright! Thank you to Danielle Felton, who was an amazing and gracious first contact at The Author Incubator; Madeline Kosten, who guided me through the initial rocky waters; and my editor Natasa Smirnov – I couldn't have done this without your amazing support, talent, and encouragement. The whole team, from finance to design, were easy and fun to work with.

I'd like to thank Lynette Smith Photography for the amazing photo shoot experience and the fabulous author photo included in this book. Her talented team, hair stylist Mirian Sanchez and makeup artist Nelisa Gomez, put me at ease and helped me look and feel beautiful.

My library is almost 100 percent nonfiction books. Books have always been my go-to when I have been faced with a problem or challenge. So, I'd like to take moment to thank the authors who supported me through the years with the words, stories, and wisdom they shared: Marsha Sinetar, Barbara Sher, Barbara Brennan, Stephen Cope, Laurence G. Boldt, Dr. Edith Eva Eger, Elle Luna, Marsha M. Lineham, Steven Pressfield, Derek Sivers, Dawna Markova, Sheila Bender, Lucia Capacchione, and Barbara Winter, who recently passed away and was not only an entrepreneur and author but also a close friend.

Although both of my parents are gone, I'd like to thank them both in heaven. My father fostered in me a lifelong love of books and learning and my mother inspired me to never give up, to love fiercely and without judgment, and to stand up and fight for what I wanted.

I'd like to thank my sister, Christine, my best friend and biggest supporter. It doesn't matter what is going on, she's always there for me, to laugh, cry, or both.

My nephews, George, Thomas, and Dylan – you

inspire me to be the very best person I can be. You each challenge me in your own unique way to look at the world with new eyes, and you give me hope for a better and brighter future for our world.

I want to express my deepest gratitude for Brandon and Sophia of Aspen Roots Energetics for their weekly healings, dream interpretations, and spiritual guidance. Their support has been invaluable on my own journey of living my very best life during some very challenging times.

I am extremely grateful for the support of Amy Wilder, certified Brennan Healing Science and integrative practitioner who has modeled for me what it means to move through this world with empathy, compassion, integrity, and joy and who has helped me reclaim my dreams.

There have been so many friends over the years, many who may have come and gone, that have impacted my life in ways that are hard to measure. I'm going to give it a try and give a shout out to a few people who helped me become the person I am today: Rose, Dawn, Jami, Michelle, Dan, Terri, Lara, Janet, the Ripple Foundation community, my classmates and teachers at the Barbara Brennan School of Healing, and Tye.

And, finally to Bob, my husband, who loved me despite how many times I changed my mind, changed jobs, careers, and majors; went off in a million different directions; started and stopped new projects almost every day; battled depression and anxiety; and pretty much drove him crazy daily and who, after living his entire life in New Jersey, picked up and moved three thousand miles across the country in 2016 so I could follow my dreams. He unexpectedly passed at the end of 2022 just as I was working to finish this book. He was my very best friend, lover, confidant, protector, and supporter. He supported my dreams and always gave me room to try, fail, and succeed. We cocreated a life together that we both loved, and I'll continue to expand and live my dreams because of the life we had together. I'm going to continue writing, teaching, coaching, traveling, creating, and reaching out to support as many people as I can to take back their own dreams, regain control of their time, and create the life they want before it's too late.

# ABOUT THE AUTHOR

Sandy Dempsey is a former executive now living the life of her dreams as an entrepreneur, transformative life coach, and energy healer. She works with women in midlife who have dedicated themselves to their families, communities, and careers for years and who are ready to reclaim their dreams. She helps them prioritize what's important to them, regain control of their time, and create an action plan to build the life they want before it's too late.

Sandy is uniquely suited to helping these over-achieving, busy, successful women create a clear vision of their dream lives and the action plans to achieve it as she has been doing the same thing for herself and her clients for years.

Sandy has had more jobs and side hustles than a dozen people combined. She has been successful in four distinct and different careers and has worked in retail, manufacturing, health care, logistics, operations, transportation, finance, and agriculture. She's spoken at national trade shows and been a guest on expert panels. As her own boss, she's sold products online, published a newsletter, consulted with small business owners, taught classes and led workshops, created events, and worked in private practice as a life coach and energy healer.

In each position, from entry level to executive and entrepreneur, she learned something about herself. Never one to sit on the sidelines and settle, she took what she learned and what she loved about each and expanded her vision of what she wanted to do and how she wanted to live her life.

Sandy knows what it's like to be busy and overwhelmed. In addition to working full time and running her own businesses, she's been a full-time caregiver. She had to learn how to prioritize what was important to her and regain control of her time so she wouldn't be consumed by these roles. She focused on a bigger vision for her life and continuously created and re-created what it meant to live her very best life. She can relate to her clients and shares her experience so they, too, can focus on their dreams and create a full and exciting life that integrates all their interests, gifts, and talents, bringing them a depth of joy and fulfillment they've never known.

Sandy's love of learning and focus on personal development led her to receive her Life Coach Certification from the Life Purpose Institute in 2020. After years of intensive study, she will graduate in June 2023 from the Barbara Brennan School of Healing, the only international, four-year training program for healers.

As a Transformative Life Purpose Coach & Energy Healer, Sandy shares her own experiences and knowledge with her clients to help them define, create, and manifest a full and exciting life as they move from feeling stuck and overwhelmed to having a plan and living the life they've always wanted.

Sandy works with clients both in-person at her office in East Wenatchee, Washington, and online via Zoom. She travels and teaches her life-changing workshops around the United States.

# ABOUT DIFFERENCE PRESS

Difference Press is the publishing arm of The Author Incubator, an Inc. 500 award-winning company that helps business owners and executives grow their brand, establish thought leadership, and get customers, clients, and highly-paid speaking opportunities, through writing and publishing books.

While traditional publishers require that you already have a large following to guarantee they make money from sales to your existing list, our approach is focused on using a book to grow your following – even if you currently don't have a following. This is why we charge an up-front fee but never take a percentage of revenue you earn from your book.

## ☞ MORE THAN A COACH. MORE THAN A PUBLISHER. ✍

We work intimately and personally with each of our authors to develop a revenue-generating strategy for the book. By using a Lean Startup style methodology, we guarantee the book's success before we even start writing. We provide all the technical support authors need with editing, design, marketing, and publishing, the emotional support you would get from a book coach to help you manage anxiety and time constraints, and we serve as a strategic thought partner engineering the book for success.

The Author Incubator has helped almost 2,000 entrepreneurs write, publish, and promote their non-fiction books. Our authors have used their books to gain international media exposure, build a brand and marketing following, get lucrative speaking engagements, raise awareness of their product or service, and attract clients and customers.

## ☞ ARE YOU READY TO WRITE A BOOK? ✍

As a client, we will work with you to make sure your book gets done right and that it gets done quickly. The Author Incubator provides one-stop for strategic book consultation, author coaching to manage writer's block and anxiety, full-service professional editing, design, and self-publishing services, and book marketing and launch campaigns. We sell this as one package so our clients are not slowed down with contradictory advice. We have a 99 percent success rate with nearly all of our clients completing their books, publishing them, and reaching bestseller status upon launch.

☞ APPLY NOW AND BE OUR NEXT SUCCESS STORY ✍

To find out if there is a significant ROI for you to write a book, get on our calendar by completing an application at www.TheAuthorIncubator.com/apply.

# OTHER BOOKS BY DIFFERENCE PRESS

*The Profitable Startup: Launch On-Time, Delight Customers and Investors, and Generate Profit Fast* by Elissa Bordner

*Outside in Recovery: Dancing My Way Back to My Self after Breast Cancer* by Jenny C. Cohen

*Why the F\*#@ Am I Still Not Organized?: Stop Struggling with Clutter Once and for All* by Star Hansen

*Stop Getting Triggered in Mediation: The Art of Managing Triggers as a Mediator and Increasing Your Impact* by Tamir Hasan

*Help Your Child Fight Cancer: A Nurse's Guide to Getting Through Every Parent's Worst Nightmare* by Amy G. Kohler

*Morning Cup of Jo: Proof That Love and Life Never Die in a Sacred Conversation between a Medical Doctor and Her Son in Spirit* by Shaunna Menard, MD

*The Quiet Quitting Nurse: 8 Steps to Help You Decide Whether or Not to Leave Your Job* by Maricea Muhammad, RN, MSN, MHA, UZIY

*Lead by Design: Applying Human Design Principles to Leadership Strategies* by Kristin Panek

*7-Figure Goddess: Making the Leap from Six to Seven Figures in Two Years (Or Less)* by Elizabeth Purvis

*Alcohol Made Me Do It: Why People Act Out of Character When They Drink and How to Stop* by Amy Turk

*Her First Place: The Black Woman's Guide to Building Generational Wealth as a First-Time Home Buyer* by J. René Walker

# THANK YOU

Wow, you made it all the way to the end. I'm honored that you took this journey with me.

## FREE GIFT

I have a surprise you will love – a companion work-book that has all the exercises and journal questions included in this book, plus tons of fun bonus material to explore. Please go to 7PathwaysHealingArts.com/TheWorkbook to download it today.

## APPLY FOR A FREE STRATEGY SESSION

If you find yourself feeling stuck, or moving forward more slowly than you expected, I can help. Go to 7path-wayshealingarts.com to book a session. Don't second guess yourself or be afraid to reach out. If you feel the impulse, do it.

I've shared tools that you can use to reclaim your dreams, prioritize your purpose, regain control of your time, and begin creating the life you want before it's too late.

I'd love to hear about how you are taking back your dreams, regaining control of your time, and creating the life you want. Contact me at 7PathwaysHealingArts.com or comment at www.Facebook.com/7Pathways HealingArts.

I believe in YOU.

Sandy Dempsey, CLC

Sandy@7PathwaysHealingArts.com

Made in United States
Troutdale, OR
11/26/2024

24910980R00100